Great Power

*Life*Themes

S E R I E S

Great Power

A 31-Day Devotional

J.I. PACKER
COMPILED BY
BETH NETHERY FEIA

VB
VINE
BOOKS

SERVANT PUBLICATIONS
ANN ARBOR, MICHIGAN

Vine Books is an imprint of Servant Publications especially designed to serve evangelical Christians.

Scripture used in the work, unless otherwise indicated, is taken from the HOLY BIBLE: NEW INTERNATIONAL VERSION® (NIV®) © 1973, 1978, 1984 International Bible Society. Used by permission of Zondervan Bible Publishers. Excerpts from *Concise Theology: A Guide to Historic Christian Beliefs* © 1993 by Foundation for Reformation used by permission of Tyndale House Publishers, Inc. All rights reserved. Excerpts from *Growing in Christ*, © 1994 by J.I. Packer used by permission of Good News Publishers/Crossway Books, Wheaton, Ill. 60187. Excerpts from *Knowing Christianity*, © 1995 by J.I. Packer used by permission of Harold Shaw Publishers, Wheaton, Ill. 60189. Excerpts from *Rediscovering Holiness*, © 1992 by J.I. Packer used by permission of Servant Publications. Excerpts from *Good News for All Seasons*, ed. Richard Allen Bodey, © 1987 by Baker Book House used by permission of Baker Book House. Excerpts from *God Has Spoken*, © 1979, 1993 by J.I. Packer used by permission of Baker Book House. Excerpts from *God's Words*, © 1988 by J.I. Packer used by permission of Baker Book House. Excerpts from *Knowing God*, © 1973 by J.I. Packer used by permission of InterVarsity Press, P.O. Box 1400, Downers Grove, Ill. 60515. All rights reserved.

Published by Servant Publications
P.O. Box 8617
Ann Arbor, Michigan 48107

Cover photograph: © R. Watts/Westlight. Used by permission.

97 98 99 00 01 10 9 8 7 6 5 4 3 2 1

Printed in the United States of America
ISBN 1-56955-084-0

LIBRARY OF CONGRESS CATALOGING-IN-PUBLICATION DATA

Packer, J.I. (James Innell)
Great power : a 31-day devotional / J.I. Packer ; compiled by Beth Nethery Feia.
   p.   cm.   — (LifeThemes series)
Includes bibliographical references.
ISBN 1-56955-084-0 (alk. paper)
1. God—Attributes—Meditations.   2. Devotional calendars.   I. Feia, Beth.   II. Title.
III. Series.
BT 130.P33   1998
231'.4—dc21   97-49138
                                                                CIP

Contents

To the Reader

When a man says of a woman, "She's done it again!" he is not always being complimentary. But when I say those words, as I now do, of Beth Feia, I am expressing the highest admiration. This is the second monthly devotional that she has crafted from pieces of Packer. *Great Grace* came first, and was brilliantly done, and I say the same of this second set of selections. So thank you, Beth!

The pieces are for meditation; that is, thought before the Lord. A meditation is a meal for the soul. With meals for the body, you first ingest (that is, take in food and drink by mouth, as physicians would say) and then digest (which means that your stomach extracts the energizing nourishment before the ingested matter is let go). You digest better if you do not gobble your food and take time to relax after the meal. In meditation the pattern is similar. Reverent reading of the text of Scripture is like going through a menu or surveying a smorgasbord in a restaurant: truths on which to meditate are there set before you. You deliberately take into your mind whatever appetizing truth you have selected. You roll it around, look at it from all angles, dissect and reassemble it, and squeeze out its application to your life: thus you digest it and absorb its message into your heart. Take your time; it pays. In restaurants, waiters come up and ask, "how is everything?" and you tell them; in meditation, we are made to realize again and again that God is near, asking us, "how is everything?"—what are we seeing, and feeling, and discerning, and deciding, as his truth gets to us?—and it is then for us to tell him, by moving from meditation to prayer and praise. The hymns that close each extract are meant to help us to do this.

Let me ask: do you sing hymns in your prayer time? Do you at least recite them? Do you actually pray out loud? The modern habit of calling personal prayer sessions Quiet Times has perhaps misled some into thinking that we should be quiet as mice—totally noiseless—when we pray. A quiet heart is certainly the hoped-for end product, and maybe this is what the phrase is pointing to, but anyone who knows what it is to become vocal before the Lord in private, lipping one's prayer at least, and sometimes singing and even shouting, will tell you that that is the way to go. Try it, anyway, and settle the matter for yourself.

Another way to think of these extracts is to see them as the spiritual equivalent of sunglasses. We wear sunglasses so that when we look toward the sun we will not be dazzled in a way that would be bad for our eyes, but will be able to see, clearly and comfortably, all we are looking at—the rising or setting sun, maybe, and the landscape flanking it. In the same way, these extracts are meant to keep us from dazzling distortions that are really forms of blindness and to mediate a biblically focused glimpse of the glory that is God's and that shines forth in all that he does. Today, the word "God" is up for grabs; anyone can define it any way they like and it means many different things to different people. Thus, some think God lacks love, because he does not insulate us from trouble (he never said he would, rather the reverse); others think he lacks wisdom and strength, as if he wants to insulate us and all mankind from trouble but is not able to manage it; and New Agers think of him as a non-personal universal presence, permeating the world as does the air—which makes God appear as a life-sustaining *it* rather than a caring, communicating, life-transforming *he*; let alone a majestic triune *they*, as in the New Testament! Clarity in your vision of God will, I hope, come your way as you brood through this material.

So may God use this book to meet and touch you as you use it in seeking to meet and touch him; and to him be praise and glory forever. Amen.

J.I. Packer

1

The Joy of Knowing God

Knowing God! Is there any greater theme to study? Is there any nobler goal at which to aim? Is there any greater good to enjoy? Is there any deeper longing in the human heart than the desire to know God? Surely not. And Christianity's good news is that it can happen! That is why the Christian message is a word for the world. To know God is the biggest and best of the blessings promised in the gospel, and to know God is celebrated in the Scriptures as the supreme gift of grace. Jeremiah, looking forward to what God was going to do, spoke in these terms: "'The time is coming,' declares the Lord, 'when I will make a new covenant with the house of Israel.'" And the consequence will be this: "No longer will a man teach his neighbor, or a man his brother, saying, 'Know the Lord,' because they will all know me, from the least of them to the greatest" (Jeremiah 31:31, 34). The fulfillment of this promise is the glory of Christianity. Christians know God. Everyone may know God.

Jesus Christ came as a preacher of eternal life. On one occasion, in prayer to his Father, he defined eternal life. "Now this is eternal life," he said, "that they may know you, the only true God, and Jesus Christ, whom you have sent" (John 17:3). The apostle John, the beloved disciple who leaned on Jesus' breast at the Last Supper and perhaps saw deeper into Jesus' heart of love than anyone, sums up at the end of his first letter what Christ has brought to him and his fellow believers: "We know also that the Son of God has come and has given us understanding, so that we may know him who is true" (1 John 5:20). "True" here means not only truthful and trustworthy as opposed to deceitful and unreliable, but also "real" as opposed to imaginary. John is telling us that Christians know—that is, are consciously and cognitively related to—the personal mind and power that is behind everything; and this knowledge is itself a personal relationship, knowledge-in-union and knowledge-in-fellowship, a precious reality of experience for which "eternal life" is the proper name. So he continues: "And we are in him who is true—even in his Son Jesus Christ. He is the true God and eternal life" (v. 20).

Such is the glorious reality of knowing God. For this we were made, and for this we have been redeemed. This is the true object of the world's longing and the sum and substance of the Christian's ambition and hope. The apostle Paul states his own life-goal in these terms: "I want to know Christ" (Philippians 3:10). The hope to which Paul looks forward he sums up in this way: "Now I know in part; then I shall know fully, even as I am fully known" (1 Corinthians 13:12). Paul's ambition and his hope are focused in terms of the knowledge of God. As for him, so for us: it is our highest dignity, our proper purpose, and our final fulfillment to know God. There is, I repeat, no more vital subject that any of us can ever explore than knowing God, according to the Scriptures.

Knowing Christianity, pp.1–3

꩜

Be thou my vision, O Lord of my heart;

Naught be all else to me, save that thou art:

Thou my best thought, by day or by night,

Waking or sleeping, thy presence my light.

Riches I heed not, nor man's empty praise,

Thou mine inheritance, now and always:

Thou and thou only first in my heart,

High King of heaven, my treasure thou art.

꩜

ANCIENT IRISH; TR. BY MARY BYRNE,
VERSIFIED BY ELEANOR HULL

2

To Know Him Is to Adore Him

Knowledge of God, according to Calvin and the Bible, is more than knowing *about* God, although knowing about God is its foundation. There is a difference between knowledge by description, in which you simply gain information about something, and knowledge by acquaintance, in which you are in direct contact with that reality. The knowledge of God is by acquaintance, which is more than knowledge by description. When it comes to knowledge by description, Calvin is very emphatic as to what must be known about God. In the very first chapter of the very first edition of the *Institutes,* Calvin wrote that there are four things that must be known about God. First, God is "infinite wisdom, righteousness, goodness, mercy, truth, power and life, so that there is no other wisdom, righteousness, goodness, mercy, truth, power and life save in him." Second, "All things, both in heaven and earth, were created to his glory." Third, "He is a righteous judge who sternly punishes those who swerve from his laws and do not wholly fulfill his will." And fourth, "He is mercy and gentleness, receiving kindly the rich and the poor who flee to his clemency and entrust themselves to his faithfulness." These are the basics we must know about God if ever we are to come to know him. But, says Calvin, to know these things and to have them clear in our minds is not yet to know God. For knowledge of God, *cognitio Dei,* is relational knowledge, knowledge that comes to us in the relationship of commitment, trust, and reliance: in other words, of faith.

Knowing God is in fact more than knowing God. It involves

knowing ourselves as needy creatures and lost sinners: for it is precisely a matter of knowing God in his saving relationship to us, that relationship in which he takes pity on us in our ill-desert and lovingly gives himself and his gifts to us for our renewal and enrichment. In other words, knowledge of God occurs only where there is knowledge of ourselves and our need and thankful reception of God's gifts to meet our need. Calvin is right! The knowledge of God and of ourselves—these two things—do in truth make up the sum of our wisdom. In fact, we do not begin to know God until we know God's gracious gift of a Savior offered to us in our weakness, sin, and wretchedness. For God is not a passive object that we can inspect and examine when and as we wish; he is an active subject who relates to us, not on our terms, but on his. And his terms are that we must be realistic about ourselves and approach him in conscious unworthiness, as drowning souls begging for a lifeline. Only to those who approach him so does he give himself covenantally and relationally; only they, therefore, come to know God.

This brings us to the point where we can speak positively of what knowing God is, and we can now declare that knowing God by faith according to the Scriptures is three things together: it is *apprehension* of who and what he is; it is *application* to ourselves of what he gives; and it is *adoration* of him, the Giver. Let Calvin say this to us in his own terms: "The knowledge of God, as I understand it, is that by which we not only conceive, that is, form the concept of there being a God, but we also grasp what benefits us, what profits us, from his giving. Nor shall we say that God is, strictly speaking, known where there is no religion or godliness." Calvin delineates here the response of humble adoration and worship by lip, by heart, and in life. Again, Calvin says this: "We are called to a knowledge of God which does not just flit about in the brain"—that is, rest content with bare notions and empty speculations. Knowledge of God, he says, is not merely a matter of ideas, but it is a knowledge which, if we rightly grasp it and allow it to take root in our hearts, will be "solid" and "fruitful." By "solid" he means firmly anchored and fixed; by "fruitful" he means "life-changing." So true knowledge of God means bringing forth the fruit of Christlikeness. Again he says: "The knowledge of God is not identified with cold speculation, but brings with it worship of him"(see *Inst.* I.ii.).

Knowing Christianity, pp.6–9

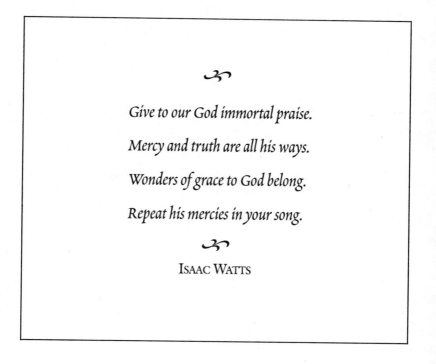

Give to our God immortal praise.

Mercy and truth are all his ways.

Wonders of grace to God belong.

Repeat his mercies in your song.

ISAAC WATTS

3

God Speaks to Us Through His Creation

How does this knowledge of God come about? What are the means of our knowing God? The usual Christian formula is that knowledge of God depends upon God's special, gracious, saving revelation of himself to us: in other words, that our knowledge and God's revelation are correlative, the former deriving from the latter. That is right. Yet sometimes I find myself wishing that in place of that word *revelation* we could form the habit of substituting another word which I think in modern discussion and debate would express more. In place of "revelation" I would like to say "communication." The word *revelation* suggests to modern minds little more than a general display or exhibition of something. I believe it is very important when we think of the revelation of God always to keep in view its nature as personal communication from the Creator to his creatures.

Communication suggests someone approaching us, coming close to us, speaking to us, telling us about himself, opening his mind to us, giving us what he has, telling us what he knows, asking for our attention, and seeking our response to what he is saying. This is the true idea of divine revelation, on which we must always keep our minds clear.

At this point, however, there is a specific problem at which we have hinted already. God made the human race in order that he might communicate himself to us and draw us into loving fellowship with himself. This was always his purpose. But we have turned away from God; sin has come in; human nature has become twisted. The human race is now radically anti-God in all its basic attitudes. Mankind is not interested in fellowship with God. It is no longer in our nature to love God or to respond to God in any kind of worship. We have our backs to God, we might say. In consequence of the fall, it is now human nature to do over and over what Adam and Eve are found doing in Genesis 3, that is, hiding from God so as to avoid having to face our guilt and to establish independence of him in the way we live. We treat ourselves as though we were God. We live for ourselves; we are self-servers; we seek to bend everything to our own interests. In doing this we fight God—the real God. We say no to him. We push him away from the center of our life to its circumference. We keep him at bay because it is our nature to do that. So God's communication to us in our sin has to do more than simply present truth to our mind. It has to work in the human heart and alter fallen human nature.

Let us back up a moment. There is, says Calvin, a universal self-communication by God, a divine reality usually called "general revelation," in the created order around us. And in our own nature, too, in our awareness of our own awesomely complex makeup and in the functioning of our consciences, there is revelation, that is, communication from God. Some sense of the reality of God and his claims comes through to us in the same way that an awareness of light comes through. It is immediate, pervasive, inescapable, undeniable. Calvin is very strong on this. "God has so shown himself in the whole workmanship of this world that men cannot open their eyes without being forced to see him." Again, "The orderly arrangement of the world is like a mirror in which we may contemplate the otherwise invisible God." Once more: "The world is created for the display of God's glory." And, "The world is the theater of God's glory." Again, "The Lord clearly displays both himself and his immortal kingdom in the mirror of his works." And yet again, "In the splendor of the heavens there is presented to our view a lively image of God" (see *Inst.* I.v.1-2).

The awareness of the Creator, then, comes through in all our commerce with his creatures, as it does in all our knowledge and awareness of ourselves and our own identity, and in the judgments on us of our conscience, and in many of the thoughts of our own hearts. But humanity's way is to ignore or deny this awareness, or, if we cannot deny it outright, to distort it and turn it into darkness and superstition. Thus the world, for all its fancied wisdom and multiple dreamed-up theologies, does not know God, even though this general communication of God through nature and inward experience is a reality for everyone. So says Calvin, following Paul, who said it before him (see Romans 1:18-23, 32; 2:12-16; 1 Corinthians 1:21). If, therefore, God is ever to be acknowledged, worshiped, and trusted as he should be, he not only must set his truth before us, but must give us eyes to see it, ears to hear it, and hearts to receive it. Which, in fact, is precisely his agenda.

Knowing Christianity, pp.9–12

The spacious firmament on high,
With all the blue ethereal sky,
And spangled heavens, a shining frame,
Their great Original proclaim;
The unwearied sun, from day to day,
Does his Creator's power display,
And publishes to every land
The work of an almighty hand.

Soon as the evening shades prevail,
The moon takes up the wondrous tale;
And nightly, to the listening earth,
Repeats the story of her birth;
Whilst all the stars that round her burn,
And all the planets in their turn,
Confirm the tidings as they roll,
And spread the truth from pole to pole.

What though in solemn silence all
Move round the dark terrestrial ball?
What though no real voice nor sound
Amidst their radiant orbs be found?
In reason's ear they all rejoice,
And utter forth a glorious voice;
Forever singing, as they shine,
"The hand that made us is divine."

JOSEPH ADDISON

4

God Speaks to Us Through His Grace

What God has done is to add to this general communication of himself in the natural order a special communication of himself in grace. In this process three stages need to be distinguished. Stage one was achieving *redemption in history*. By words and by works God made himself known on the stage of history in saving action. The words were basic, for first God declared what he was going to do; then, after making the announcement, he acted, fulfilling his word and doing what he said. That is how it was at the Exodus, when he saved Israel out of captivity in Egypt. That is what he did when in the fullness of time he sent his own Son, born of a woman, to redeem those who were under the law, sinners like you and me, so that we might receive the gift of adoption and so become children in his family.

Stage two was recording *revelation in writing*. That was the work of God inspiring the Holy Scriptures. God caused to be written interpretive records of what he had said and done, so that all generations might know of the redemptive revelation in history that he had made. The written record is our Bible, which has Jesus Christ the Redeemer as its central focus.

The third stage in the communicative process is securing *reception by individuals* of the realities of redemption declared in the Scriptures, a reception that becomes a reality through the work of the Holy Spirit. God's word to the world is the message of new life in Christ. The Holy Spirit opens hearts to give this word entrance and renews hearts so that we might turn around again to face God.

We thus become new creatures in Christ. When the New Testament speaks of God revealing himself to human beings, it is this third stage in the process of divine communication that is in view. When Jesus said, "…no one knows the Father except the Son and those to whom the Son chooses to reveal him" (Matthew 11:27), he had in mind the enlightening impact of his teaching through the Holy Spirit. And it appears that when Jesus said, "Blessed are you, Simon son of Jonah, for this [my identity as God's Christ] was not revealed to you by man, but by my Father in heaven" (Matthew 16:17), he meant that Simon had been enlightened to see the meaning of things he had heard Jesus say and seen him do during the previous months. Paul uses the word *reveal* in the same way when he says in Galatians that God "was pleased to reveal his Son in me" (Galatians 1:15-16). The words "in me" mean, in a way that convinced Paul's heart. Paul lost his sight physically for a few days but gained his sight spiritually forever. The truth about Jesus, risen Savior and Lord, had been told him before, but he had been blind to it; now the eyes of his heart were opened, and he saw. The same thought is being expressed by Paul in other words when he says in 2 Corinthians 4:6 that "God, who said, 'Let light shine out of darkness,' made his light shine in our hearts to give us the light of the knowledge of the glory of God in the face of Christ." Often this third stage of God's revelatory work is called illumination. John expresses it in words that we quoted earlier: "the Son of God … has given us understanding, so that we may know him who is true" (1 John 5:20).

Do you see now that stage two in the process, the inspiring of the Bible, is absolutely crucial? Calvin regularly referred to the Bible as the "oracles of God," a phrase lifted from Romans 3:2, that the NIV renders as "the very words of God." Calvin took it and used it again and again to express the thought that what we have in Scripture is God's own witness to his work of salvation. Calvin's view is that the Bible through the Spirit has a double function in relation to us sin-blinded sinners. It functions both as our school-master, teaching us the truth, operating as the rule for our own teaching and speaking, and also as our spectacles, enabling us to see God clearly.

Calvin's illustration speaks much to me because I am nearsighted. If I take off my glasses, I cannot see anything or anyone clearly. I can see only a set of smudges. Calvin, who himself was nearsighted, says, in effect, that the natural person without the Scriptures has no more than a smudgy awareness that there is a divine something or some-one there; he or she does not know, however, who the something or someone is. But when nearsighted persons put on their glasses, then they see clearly what before was only a smudge; and when we begin to study the Scriptures, we begin to see clearly him of whom we had that unclear awareness. The Scriptures serve us as glasses, focusing for us and in us our awareness of God and showing us precisely who and what this God is.

Knowing Christianity, pp.12–15

ॐ

Blessed Jesus, at thy word,

We are gathered all to hear thee;

Let our hearts and souls be stirred

Now to seek and love and fear thee,

By thy teachings sweet and holy,

Drawn from earth to love thee solely.

All our knowledge, sense, and sight

Lie in deepest darkness shrouded

Till thy Spirit breaks our night

With the beams of truth unclouded.

Glorious Lord, thyself impart,

Light of Light, from God proceeding,

Open thou each mind and heart,

Help us by thy Spirit's pleading.

ॐ

TOBIAS CLAUSNITZER
TR. CATHERINE WINKWORTH

5

A Panoramic View of God's Attributes

God is personal and triune. God is always Three-in-One and One-in-Three. All three are equal in power and glory, and in all divine acts all three persons are involved. God is as truly three personal centers in a relationship of mutual love as he is a single personal deity. "He" when used of God means "they"—the Father, the Son, and the Holy Spirit.

God is self-existent and self-sufficient. God does not have it in him, either in purpose or in power, to stop existing. He exists necessarily. The answer to the child's question "Who made God?" is that God did not need to be made, since he was always there. He depends on nothing outside himself but is at every point self-sustaining.

God is simple, perfect, and immutable. This means he is wholly and totally involved in everything that he is and does. His nature, goals, plans, and ways of acting do not change, either for the better (being perfect, he cannot become better than he is) or for the worse.

God is infinite, without body, all-present, all-knowing, and eternal. God is not bound by any of the limitations of space or time that apply to us, his creatures, in our body-anchored existence. Instead, he is always present everywhere, though invisibly and imperceptibly. He is at every moment cognizant of everything that ever was, or now is, or shall be.

God is purposeful and all-powerful. He has a plan for the history of the universe, and in executing it he governs and controls all created realities. Without violating the nature of things, and without at any stage infringing upon human free will, God acts in, with, and through his creatures to do everything that he wishes to do exactly as he wishes to do it. By this sovereign, overruling action he achieves his goals.

God is both transcendent over and immanent in his world. On the one hand, he is distinct from the world, does not need it, and exceeds the grasp of any created intelligence that is found in it. On the other hand, he permeates the world in sustaining and creative power, shaping and steering it in a way that keeps it on its planned course.

God is impassible. This means that no one can inflict suffering, pain, or any sort of distress on him. Insofar as God enters into an experience of suffering, it is through empathy for his creatures and according to his own deliberate decision. He is never his creatures' victim. This impassibility has not been taken by the Christian mainstream to mean that God is a stranger to joy and delight; rather, it asserts the permanence of God's joy, which no pain, however real, can cloud.

God is love. Giving out of good will, for the recipient's benefit, is the abiding quality both of ongoing relationships within the Trinity and of God's relationship with his creatures. This love is qualified by holiness (purity), a further facet of God's character that finds expression in his abhorrence and rejection of moral evil.

God is eternally worthy of our praise, loyalty, and love. God's ways with mankind, as set forth in Scripture, show him to be both awesome and adorable by reason of his truthfulness, faithfulness, grace, mercy, patience, constancy, wisdom, justice, goodness, and generosity. The ultimate purpose of human life is to render to him worship and service, in which both he and we will find joy. This is what we were made for and what we are saved for. This is what it means to know God and to be known by him and to glorify him.

God communicates to his creatures. God uses his gift of language, given to mankind, to tell us things directly in and through the words of his spokespersons—prophets, apostles, the incarnate Son, the writers of Holy Scripture, and those who preach the Bible. God's messages all come to us as good news of grace. They may contain particular commands, even threats or warnings, but the fact that God addresses us at all is an expression of his good will and an invitation to fellowship. The central message of Scripture, the hub of the wheel whose spokes are the various truths about God that the Bible teaches, is and always will be God's unmerited gift of salvation, freely offered to us in and by Jesus Christ.

Knowing Christianity, pp.45–48

⇛

Immortal, invisible, God only wise,
In light inaccessible hid from our eyes,
Most blessed, most glorious, the Ancient of Days,
Almighty, victorious, thy great name we praise.

Unresting, unhasting, and silent as light,
Nor wanting, nor wasting, thou rulest in might;
Thy justice like mountains high soaring above
Thy clouds which are fountains of goodness and love.

To all, life thou givest, to both great and small;
In all life thou livest, the true life of all;
We blossom and flourish as leaves on the tree,
And wither and perish, but naught changeth thee.

⇛

WALTER C. SMITH

6

The Trinity: God in Three Persons

The Bible bequeaths to the church the doctrine of three divine Agents and one God: Father, Son, and Holy Spirit as the "name"—as Karl Barth happily put it, the "Christian name"—of the one Yahweh (modern rendering of Jehovah). As the Athanasian Creed states, "the Father is Lord, the Son Lord, and the Holy Ghost Lord. And yet they are not three Lords: but one Lord." Not one person impersonating two others in addition to himself; not a trio of separate deities; but a God who is really one, and yet within whose unity there are really three, the threeness and the oneness being each fundamental to the other. The three are "in" each other without losing their personal distinctness, just as all three may be "in" the Christian without him losing his personal identity and self-awareness. They stand in definite and distinct mutual relations: the Father initiates, the Son is the Father's agent, the Spirit is the executive of both. Yet (the Athanasian Creed again) "the Godhead of the Father, of the Son, and of the Holy Ghost, is all one: the glory equal, the majesty co-eternal. Such as the Father is, such is the Son, and such is the Holy Ghost."

"So what?" says someone. "Granted, Trinitarian thinking is biblical, but is it important? What is lost by not asserting the Trinity?"

What is lost is, quite simply, the gospel—or at least, the right to assert the gospel. Let me explain.

In following a path up a mountain, you concentrate on the path rather than the mountain. A single-minded person could hurry to the top without really noticing the mountain at all. I once climbed a mountain whose name I did not discover till four years afterward. Now, when you state the gospel you take a path up a mountain: and the Trinity is both the name and the nature of the mountain you have under your feet the whole time.

In John 3:1-15 we see Jesus explaining to Nicodemus that the only way into God's kingdom is through faith in the Son whom the Father sent down to be "lifted up" in sacrificial death, and through being born anew of the Spirit. Jesus is spelling out the gospel; and its substance, very obviously, is the combined action of the Triune God. Well did the Anglican Prayer Book select John 3:1-15 as the Gospel for Trinity Sunday! The Trinity is the basis of the gospel, and the gospel is a declaration of the Trinity in action.

To put it the other way round: the gospel says that there was in God from eternity mutuality of love and joy (John 1:1ff.; 17:5, 24); that humans were made to share this fellowship; that when sin had made this impossible, God came in person—the second Person, sent by the first Person and empowered by the third Person—to save us; that God-made-flesh died for us, lives for us, unites us to himself, brings us to God the Father now and will take us one day to share his glory; that a divine Guest, the Holy Spirit, indwells each Christian (there are some two billion of us alive today, leaving aside the faithful departed) to prompt prayer and transform our fallen nature; and that Jesus Christ is companion and friend to every single believer, giving him or her constant and undistracted attention. It is surely obvious that none of these marvelous, almost fantastic things could be said save on the supposition that Father, Son, and Holy Spirit are God—in other words, that God is Father, Son, and Holy Spirit. Those who deny the Trinity have to scale down the gospel—and do.

So we may well make it a matter of conscience to pray:

Almighty and everlasting God, who hast given unto us thy servants grace by the confession of a true faith to acknowledge the glory of the eternal Trinity, and in the power of the Divine Majesty to worship the Unity; We beseech thee, that thou wouldest keep us steadfast in this faith, and evermore defend us from all adversities, who livest and reignest, one God, world without end.

Book of Common Prayer
Collect for Trinity Sunday

God's Words, pp.54–56

ঌ

Come, thou almighty King,
Help us thy name to sing,
Help us to praise:
Father, all glorious,
O'er all victorious,
Come, and reign over us,
Ancient of Days.

Come, thou Incarnate Word!
Gird on thy mighty sword;
Our prayer attend:
Come, and thy people bless,

And give thy word success;
Spirit of holiness!
On us descend.

Come, Holy Comforter,
Thy sacred witness bear
In this glad hour:
Thou who almighty art,
Now rule in every heart,
And ne'er from us depart,
Spirit of power.

To thee, great One in three,
Eternal praises be
Hence evermore.
His sov'reign majesty
May we in glory see,
And to eternity
Love and adore.

ॐ

ITALIAN HYMN

7

The Trinity:
How Three Persons Accomplish Our Salvation

God is tripersonal; the Father, the Son, and the Holy Spirit are co-equal and co-eternal, uncreated and inseparable, undivided though distinguishable. This is a truth that becomes clear when Jesus in the Gospels indicates, on the one hand, that though he is divine and to be worshiped, he is not the same person as the Father, whose will he does and to whom he prays—and then indicates, on the other hand, that the Holy Spirit, who will come as his deputy, is a further divine person on the same footing as himself. The Trinity is the linchpin of orthodox belief.

The idea of the Trinity is one of the hardest thoughts round which the human mind has ever been asked to wrap itself. It is far easier to get it wrong than to get it right.

When, however, we turn to what Jesus said to Nicodemus in John 3:1-5, we find faith in the Trinity presented in quite a different light—not now as the linchpin of orthodox belief, but as, literally and precisely, the sinner's way of salvation. How does Jesus' teaching here do this? Let me show you how.

Nicodemus, a senior Jewish ruler and theologian, a man as eminent as an archbishop, a cardinal, or a distinguished professor today, has come to meet Jesus, the novice preacher from the Galilean backwoods, who is in Jerusalem, it seems, for the first time since his ministry started. Being older, Nicodemus speaks first. His opening words are kind words, words of affirmation and welcome. "Rabbi [teacher]," he says, giving the young preacher a title of honor straight away, "we [that is, "my colleagues and I," Jerusalem's top people] know you are a teacher who has come from God. For no one could perform the miraculous signs you are doing if God were not with him" (v.2). As if to say: "I am sure, Jesus, that you are wondering whether we of the religious establishment accept you and approve of what you are doing and regard you as one of us. Well now, I am here to tell you that we do, and we shall be happy to have you as a regular member of our discussion circle (the Jerusalem Theological Society, as we might call it). Come and join us!" Such was the burden of Nicodemus' speech.

Do you see, now, what Nicodemus was doing under all that politeness? By treating Jesus as a recruit for the Jewish establishment, he was patronizing the Son of God! So Jesus does not respond by thanking Nicodemus for his kind words. He strikes a different note and tells his eminent visitor that without being born again, one cannot see the kingdom of God. When Nicodemus expresses bewilderment, Jesus amplifies his meaning in the words of our text: "I tell you the truth, no one can enter the kingdom of God unless he is born of water and the Spirit." Then he explains that natural and spiritual birth are two different things and concludes: "You should not be surprised at my saying, 'You must be born again'" (v.7).

I ask you, now, to notice two things. The first is that *there are three persons* mentioned in verse 5, which is our text. There is the "I" of "I tell you the truth," the speaker, Jesus himself—God's "One and Only," as John, in 1:14, has already called him, and as the beloved verse 16 of chapter three will call him again. There is "God," the One whom Jesus called Father and taught his disciples to call Father—God whose kingdom Jesus is announcing. And there is the Holy Spirit, through whose power in new creation one must start life all over again, if one is ever to see and enter the kingdom.

These are the three persons of the divine Trinity who are our special concern now.

The second thing I ask you to notice is that *there are three stages* in the flow of Jesus' response to Nicodemus. We may set them out as follows.

Do you want to see and enter the kingdom of God? Then you must be born again, of water and the Spirit (vv. 3-10).

What is the kingdom of God? The whole New Testament makes clear that it is not a territorial realm but a personal relationship. The kingdom exists in any life where God is made King and Jesus the Savior is acknowledged as Lord. The relationship brings salvation from sin and Satan and spiritual death. Jesus bestows forgiveness of sins, adoption into God's family, and the joy of eternal life on all who entrust their destiny to him and give him the love and loyalty of their hearts. To this new relationship, the path—the only path, as Jesus explains to Nicodemus—is new birth.

Thus Jesus lays it down that only through new birth can Nicodemus, or you, or I, or anyone else, come into the kingdom of God. This leads to the second stage in his flow of thought.

Do you want to be born again? Then you must be willing to learn from Jesus Christ (vv. 11-13).

The message to Nicodemus, and to us, is this: Believe in Jesus—that is, trust in him, rely on him, tell him that he is your only hope, embrace him as your Savior—and your sins will be forgiven, your sickness of spirit healed, and your uncleanness before God washed away. Then you will know that you, too, have been born again.

The statement of verses 14 and 15, pointing as it does to Jesus' cross as the means of our salvation, is the purest gospel, as is the beloved sixteenth verse that follows it: "For God so loved the world that he gave his one and only Son, that whoever believes in him shall not perish but have eternal life." In learning the good news from these words, we are on familiar ground. But what I am asking you to notice now is that the entire conversation with Nicodemus presents us with profound teaching about the Trinity also, by setting before us the person and work both of God's Son and of God's Spirit. Jesus, we learn, is the God-sent, divine-human sin-bearer, who by his cross secured eternal life for us. The Spirit is the divine regenerator who by transforming our inner disposition, and in that sense changing our nature, enables us to experience the life of the kingdom of God. Without the Son and the Spirit there can be no salvation for anyone.

What it amounts to, then, is that in this passage, as in many more throughout the New Testament, the truths of the Holy Trinity and of sovereign saving grace prove to be not two truths but one. The doctrine of salvation is the good news of the Father's giving us his Son to redeem us and his Spirit to renew us. The doctrine of the Trinity is the good news of three divine persons working together to raise us into spiritual life and bring us to the glory of God's kingdom.

Do not dismiss the doctrine of the Trinity as so much useless lumber for the mind. If the place of any of the three persons is misconceived or denied, the gospel falls. The gospel proclaims precisely the joint saving action of the three persons, and it is lost as soon as one's hold on their distinct divine personhood slackens.

Let the doctrine of the Trinity keep your understanding of the gospel in good shape. Let it remind you to give equal emphasis in your thinking and your witness to the sovereign initiative of the Father who planned salvation, the atoning sacrifice of the Son who obtained salvation, and the mighty power of the Spirit who applies salvation. Let it prompt you to lay equal stress on the love of each in the work of grace.

"The Trinity and the Gospel,"
Good News for All Seasons, pp.91–98

Holy Father, Holy Son,

Holy Spirit, three we name thee;

While in essence only One,

Undivided God we claim thee;

And adoring bend the knee,

While we sing our praise to thee.

GERMAN, 18TH CENTURY,
TR. CLARENCE WALWORTH

8

Almighty:
God Is All-Powerful and Ever Present

God is present in all places; we should not think of him, however, as filling spaces, for he has no physical dimensions. It is as pure spirit that he pervades all things, in a relationship of immanence that is more than we body-bound creatures can understand. One thing that is clear, however, is that he is present everywhere in the fullness of all that he is and all the powers that he has, and needy souls praying to him anywhere in the world receive the same fullness of his undivided attention. Because God is omnipresent, he is able to give his entire attention to millions of individuals at the same time. Belief in God's omnipresence, thus understood, is reflected in Psalm 139:7-10; Jeremiah 23:23-24; and Acts 17:24-28. When Paul speaks of the ascended Christ as filling all things (Ephesians 4:8), Christ's availability everywhere in the fullness of his power is certainly part of the meaning that is being expressed. It is true to say that Father, Son, and Holy Spirit are today omnipresent together, though the personal presence of the glorified Son is spiritual (through the Holy Spirit), not physical (in the body).

"I know that you can do all things; no plan of yours can be thwarted" (Job 42:2). Thus Job testifies to the almightiness (omnipotence) of God. Omnipotence means in practice the power to do everything that in his rational and moral perfection (i.e., his wisdom and goodness) God wills to do. This does not mean that God can do literally everything: he cannot sin, lie, change his nature, or deny the demands of his holy character (Numbers 23:19; 1 Samuel 15:29; 2 Timothy 2:13; Hebrews 6:18; James 1:13, 17); nor can he make a square circle, for the notion of a square circle is self-contradictory; nor can he cease to be God. But all that he wills and promises he can and will do.

Was it excessive for David to say, "I love you, O Lord, my strength. The Lord is my rock, my fortress and my deliverer; my God is my rock, in whom I take refuge. He is my shield and the horn of my salvation, my stronghold" (Psalm 18:1-2)? Was it excessive for another psalmist to declare, "God is our refuge and strength, an ever-present help in trouble" (Psalm 46:1)? Not when they knew God to be omnipresent and omnipotent, though otherwise it might have been. Knowledge of God's greatness (and his omnipresence and omnipotence are aspects of his greatness) naturally produces great faith and great praise.

Concise Theology, pp.35–36

Praise to the Lord, the Almighty, the King of creation!

O my soul, praise him, for he is thy health and salvation!

All ye who hear, now to his temple draw near;

Praise him in glad adoration!

Praise to the Lord! Who o'er all things so wondrously reigneth,

Shelters thee under his wings, yea, so gently sustaineth;

Hast thou not seen how thy entreaties have been

Granted in what he ordaineth?

Praise to the Lord! Who doth prosper thy work and defend thee;

Surely his goodness and mercy here daily attend thee.

Ponder anew what the Almighty can do,

If with his love he befriend thee.

JOACHIM NEANDER
TR. CATHERINE WINKWORTH

9

Sovereign:
Nothing Can Thwart God's Loving Will

God is the Lord, the King, the omnipotent one who reigns over his world. Note the ecstatic joy with which God's sovereign rule is proclaimed and praised in (for instance) Psalms 93, 96, 97, 99:1-5, and 103. People treat God's sovereignty as a theme for controversy, but in Scripture it is matter for worship.

We need to realize that you cannot rightly understand God's ways at any point till you see them in the light of his sovereignty. But, though the believing heart warms to it, it is not an easy truth for our minds to grasp, and a number of questions arise.

Does omnipotence mean that God can do literally anything? No, that is not the meaning. There are many things God cannot do. He cannot do what is self-contradictory or nonsensical. Nor (and this is vital) can he act out of character. God has a perfect moral character, and it is not in him to deny it. He cannot be capricious, unloving, random, unjust, or inconsistent. Just as he cannot pardon sin without atonement, because that would not be right, so he cannot fail to be "faithful and just" in forgiving sins that are confessed in faith, and in keeping all the other promises he has made, for failure here would not be right either. Moral instability, vacillation, and unreliability are marks of weakness, not of strength: but God's omnipotence is supreme strength, making it impossible that he should lapse into imperfections of this sort.

The positive way to say this is that though there are things that a holy, rational God is incapable of intending, all that he intends to do he actually does. "Whatever the Lord pleases he does" (Psalm

135:6, RSV). As, when he planned to make the world, "he spoke, and it came to be" (Psalm 33:9; see Genesis 1), so with each other thing that he wills. With men, "there's many a slip 'twixt cup and lip," but not with him.

Second, is not God's power to fulfill his purposes limited by the free will of man? No. Man's power of spontaneous and responsible choice is a created thing, an aspect of the mystery of created human nature, and God's power to fulfill his purposes is not limited by anything that he has made. Just as he works out his will through the functioning of the physical order, so he works out his will through the functioning of our psychological makeup. In no case is the integrity of the created thing affected, and it is always possible (apart from some miracles) to "explain" what has happened without reference to the rule of God. But in every case God orders the things that come to pass.

So, therefore, without violating the nature of created realities, or reducing man's activity to robot level, God still "accomplishes all things according to the counsel of his will" (Ephesians 1:11, RSV).

But surely in that case what we think of as our free will is illusory and unreal? That depends on what you mean. It is certainly illusory to think that our wills are only free if they operate apart from God. But free will in the sense of "free agency," as theologians have defined it—that is, the power of spontaneous, self-determining choice referred to above—is real. As a fact of creation, an aspect of our humanness, it exists, as all created things do, in God. How God sustains it and overrules it without overriding it is his secret; but that he does so is certain, both from our conscious experience of making decisions and acting "of our own free will," and also from Scripture's sobering insistence that we are answerable to God for our actions, just because in the moral sense they really are ours.

Third, does not the existence of evil—moral badness, useless pain, and waste of good—suggest that God the Father is not almighty after all?—for surely he would remove these things if he could? Yes, he would, and he is doing so! Through Christ, bad folk like you and me are already being made good; new pain- and disease-free bodies are on the way, and a reconstructed cosmos with them; and Paul assures us that "the sufferings of this present time are not worth comparing with the glory that is to be revealed to us" (Romans 8:18, RSV; cf. 19-23). If God moves more slowly than we wish in clearing evil out of this world and introducing the new order, that, we may be sure, is in order to widen his gracious purpose and include in it more victims of the world's evil than otherwise he could have done. (Study 2 Peter 3:3-10, especially verse 8ff.)

The truth of God's almightiness in creation, providence, and grace is the basis of all our trust, peace, and joy in God, and the safeguard of all our hopes of answered prayer, present protection, and final salvation. It means that neither fate, nor the stars, nor blind chance, nor man's folly, nor Satan's malice controls this world; instead, a morally perfect God runs it, and none can dethrone him or thwart his purposes of love.

Growing in Christ, pp.31–32

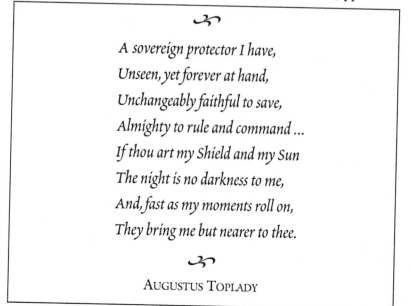

A sovereign protector I have,
Unseen, yet forever at hand,
Unchangeably faithful to save,
Almighty to rule and command ...
If thou art my Shield and my Sun
The night is no darkness to me,
And, fast as my moments roll on,
They bring me but nearer to thee.

AUGUSTUS TOPLADY

10

Creator:
God Is Our Maker and All Belongs to Him

"In the beginning God created the heavens and the earth"; so begins the Bible. ("Heavens and earth" is Bible language for "everything that is.")

It is arguable how much (or how little) Genesis 1 and 2 tell us about the *method* of creation—whether, for instance, they do or do not rule out the idea of physical organisms evolving through epochs of thousands of years. What is clear, however, is that their main aim is to tell us not how the world was made, but who made it.

The solution-chapter in one of Dorothy Sayers' detective stories is called "When You Know How You Know Who." Genesis 1 and 2, however tell us *who* without giving many answers about *how*. Some today may think this is a defect; but in the long perspective of history our present-day "scientific" preoccupation with *how* rather than *who* looks very odd in itself. Rather than criticize these chapters for not feeding our secular interest, we should take from them needed rebuke of our perverse passion for knowing Nature without regard for what matters most; namely, knowing Nature's Creator.

You have seen the sea? The sky? Sun, moon, and stars? You have watched the birds and the fish? You have observed the landscape, the vegetation, the animals, the insects, all the big things and little things together? You have marveled at the wonderful complexity of human beings, with all their powers and skills, and the deep feelings of fascination, attraction, and affection that men and women arouse in each other? Fantastic, isn't it? Well now, meet the one who is behind it all! As if to say: now that you have enjoyed these works of art, you must shake hands with the artist; since you were thrilled by the music, we will introduce you to the composer. It was to show us the Creator rather than the creation, and to teach us knowledge of God rather than physical science, that Genesis 1 and 2, along with such celebrations of creation as Psalm 104 and Job 38–41, were written.

In creating, God was craftsman and more. Craftsmen shape existing material, and are limited by it, but no material existed at all till God said "Let there be ..." To make this point, theologians speak of creation "out of nothing," meaning not that nothing was a sort of a something(!) but that God in creating was absolutely free and unrestricted, and that nothing determined or shaped what he brought into being save his own idea of what he would like.

The Creator-creature distinction is basic to the Bible view of God's lordship in providence and grace, and indeed to all true thought about God and man. That is why it is in the Creed. Its importance is at least threefold.

First, *it stops misunderstanding of God*. God made us in his image, but we tend to think of him in ours! ("Man made God in his own image" was a crack by Voltaire, rather too true to be good.) But the Creator-creature distinction reminds us that God does not depend on us as we depend on him, nor does he exist by our will and for our pleasure, nor may we think of his personal life as being just like ours. As creatures we are limited; we cannot know everything at once, nor be present everywhere, nor do all we should like to do, nor continue unchanged through the years. But the Creator is not limited in these ways. Therefore we find him *incomprehensible*—by which I mean, not *making no sense*, but *exceeding our grasp*. We can no more take his measure than our dogs and cats can take our measure.

Second, *this distinction stops misunderstanding of the world.* The world exists in its present stable state by the will and power of its Maker. Since it is his world, we are not its owners, free to do as we like with it, but its stewards, answerable to him for the way we handle its resources. And since it is his world, we must not depreciate it. Much religion has built on the idea that the material order is evil, and therefore to be refused and ignored as far as possible. This view has sometimes called itself Christian, but it is really as un-Christian as can be. For matter, being made by God, was and is *good* in his eyes (Genesis 1:31), and should be so in ours (1 Timothy 4:4). We serve God by using and enjoying temporal things gratefully, with a sense of their value to him, their Maker, and of his generosity in giving them to us.

Third, *this distinction stops misunderstanding of ourselves.* As man is not his own maker, so he may not think of himself as his own master. "God made me for himself, to serve him here." God's claim upon us is the first fact of life that we must face, and we need a healthy sense of our creaturehood to keep us facing it.

Growing in Christ, pp.35–37

ॐ

All creatures of our God and King,
Lift up your voice and with us sing
Alleluia! Alleluia!
Thou burning sun with golden beam,
Thou silver moon with softer gleam,
O praise him, O praise him!
Alleluia! Alleluia! Alleluia!

Let all things their Creator bless,
And worship him in humbleness;
O praise him! Alleluia!
Praise, praise the Father, praise the Son,
And praise the Spirit, Three in One!
O praise him, O praise him!
Alleluia! Alleluia! Alleluia!

ॐ

FRANCIS OF ASSISI
TR. WILLIAM H. DRAPER

11

Designer:
God Turned Chaos Into Order

The commonest word for "world" in the New Testament (occurring about 150 times) is *kosmos*. *Kosmos* basically means "order," and the thought of order—the harmonious integration of a variety of elements and energies—is in fact the key-thought in the biblical presentation of God's work as Creator. Note the layout of the first chapter of Genesis. Its stress is not on the fact that God made all things out of nothing (the doctrine of creation from nothing, though no doubt implicit in Genesis 1:1, derives rather from texts like Psalm 33:6; John 1:3; Colossians 1:16ff.; Hebrews 11:3). What Genesis 1 emphasizes is the fact that God by his creative Word and Spirit (speech and breath) brought order out of a primeval chaos. "The earth was without form and void, and darkness was upon the face of the deep; and the Spirit [breath] of God was moving over the face of the waters. And God said ... and there was ..." (Genesis 1:2ff., RSV). The chapter goes on to tell us how God separated land from sea, established the regular rhythm of day and night and the round of the year, filled the dry land with vegetation, and populated it with birds, beasts, and human beings, each 'according to its kind.' Everywhere, God's creative work brought *order* out of a state of affairs that otherwise would have remained chaotic. This is the central truth about God the Creator that Genesis 1 is concerned to show us.

The producing of an ordered world involved the imposing of limits and boundaries in both space and time. Each thing must be kept in its place, so that there might be room for everything that God had planned. Accordingly, in space, God restrained the rain and the sea (Genesis 1:6-10; cf. Job 38:8ff.; Psalm 104:9), so that all his purposes for life on dry land might be fulfilled. Similarly, when men multiplied, he allotted particular areas for each national group to inhabit (Deuteronomy 32:8). Again, in time, God has set bounds, not only to the life of each living thing and to the seasons of the year and the natural processes proper to each, like fruit-bearing and hibernation, but also to the successive eras of human history. We find Paul explaining to the Athenians these created, providential limits that God has imposed upon the life of mankind. "He made every nation of men, that they should inhabit the whole earth; and he determined the times set for them and the exact places where they should live" (Acts 17:26).

What God made at the beginning, then, was precisely a world-*order*. It is natural to conclude from Genesis 1 that the goodness that God saw in each thing as he formed it, and in the entire fin-ished work of creation before mankind fell, lay partly, at least, in the fact that each step in creation was a further step in the exclusion and banishment of chaos. The Creator is a God, not of confusion, but of order.

Mankind was made to rule creation. This noblest of creatures was set at the head of the created order, and told to subdue it (Genesis 1:28); that is, to map and tap its resources, to bring out and utilize its latent possibilities, to put it to work for him, and thus to harness and develop all its powers for the enriching of his own life, in obedi-ence to God. God gave us richly all things to enjoy. He willed to be glorified through humanity's learning to appreciate and admire his wisdom and goodness as Creator. In other words, God commis-sioned mankind to build a culture and civilization.

Right at the outset, God introduced Adam to the vocation

appointed for him by putting him in charge of a garden (Genesis 2:15). Gardening is a perfect picture of the human cultural task. Adam was to learn to see the whole created order as, so to speak, the estate that he, as God's gardener, was responsible for cultivating. Man was not made to be a barbarian, nor to live in savagery, and "back to nature" is never the road back to Eden. For mankind was made to rule nature, to master it and to enjoy its fruits, to the glory of God the Creator, according to the principle laid down in 1 Timothy 4:4: "For everything God created is good, and nothing is to be rejected if it is received with thanksgiving." So the psalmist writes: "What is man that thou art mindful of him, and the son of man that thou visitest him? For thou hast made him a little lower than the angels, and hast crowned him with glory and honor. Thou madest him to have dominion over the works of thy hands; thou hast put all things under his feet" (Psalm 8:4-6, KJV).

God's Words, pp.58–61

꒰

Praise the Lord, ye heavens, adore him;
Praise him, angels, in the height;
Sun and moon, rejoice before him,
Praise him, all ye stars of light.
Praise the Lord, for he hath spoken;
Worlds his mighty voice obeyed;
Laws which never shall be broken
For their guidance hath he made.

꒰

BASED ON PSALM 148
FOUNDLING HOSPITAL "COLLECTION," C.1801

12

Providence:
God Is Completely in Charge of His World

If Creation was a unique exercise of divine energy causing the world to be, providence is a continued exercise of that same energy whereby the Creator, according to his own will, *(a)* keeps all creatures in being, *(b)* involves himself in all events, and *(c)* directs all things to their appointed end. The model is of purposive personal management with total "hands-on" control: God is completely in charge of his world. His hand may be hidden, but his rule is absolute.

Some have restricted God's providence to foreknowledge without control, or upholding without intervention, or general oversight without concern for details, but the testimony to providence as formulated above is overwhelming.

The Bible clearly teaches God's providential control
- *over the universe at large;*
- *over the physical world;*
- *over the brute creation;*
- *over the affairs of nations;*
- *over man's birth and lot in life;*
- *over the outward successes and failures of men's lives;*
- *over things seemingly accidental or insignificant;*
- *in the protection of the righteous;*
- *in supplying the wants of God's people;*
- *in giving answers to prayer;*
- *in the exposure and punishment of the wicked.* *

* L. Berkhof, *Systematic Theology*, 4th ed.

Clear thinking about God's involvement in the world-process and in the acts of rational creatures requires complementary sets of statements, thus: a person takes action, or an event is triggered by natural causes, or Satan shows his hand—yet God overrules. This is the message of the book of Esther, where God's name nowhere appears. Again: things that are done contravene God's will of command—yet they fulfill his will of events (Ephesians 1:11). Again: humans mean what they do for evil—yet God who overrules uses their actions for good (Genesis 50:20; Acts 2:23). Again: humans, under God's overruling, sin—yet God is not the author of sin (James 1:13-17); rather, he is its judge.

The nature of God's "concurrent" or "confluent" involvement in all that occurs in his world, as—without violating the nature of things, the ongoing causal processes, or human free agency—he makes his will of events come to pass, is mystery to us, but the consistent biblical teaching about God's involvement is as stated above.

Of the evils that infect God's world (moral and spiritual perversity, waste of good, and the physical disorders and disruptions of a spoiled cosmos), it can summarily be said: God permits evil (Acts 14:16); he punishes evil with evil (Psalm 81:11-12; Romans 1:26-32); he brings good out of evil (Genesis 50:20; Acts 2:23; 4:27-28; 13:27; 1 Corinthians 2:7-8); he uses evil to test and discipline those he loves (Matthew 4:1-11; Hebrews 12:4-14); and one day he will redeem his people from the power and presence of evil altogether (Revelations 21:27; 22:14-15).

The doctrine of providence teaches Christians that they are never in the grip of blind forces (fortune, chance, luck, fate); all that happens to them is divinely planned, and with each event comes a new summons to trust, obey, and rejoice, knowing that all is for one's spiritual and eternal good (Romans 8:28).

Concise Theology, pp. 54–56

Neither life nor death shall ever
From the Lord his children sever;
Unto them his grace he showeth,
And their sorrows all he knoweth.

Praise the Lord in joyful numbers,
Your Protector never slumbers;
At the will of your Defender
Ev'ry foeman must surrender.

Though he giveth or he taketh,
God his children ne'er forsaketh;
His the loving purpose solely
To preserve them pure and holy.

More secure is no one ever
Than the loved ones of the Savior;
Not yon star on high abiding
Nor the bird in homenest hiding.

LINA SANDELL

13

Transcendence:
Our Infinite God Upholds Everything

"God is spirit," said Jesus to the Samaritan woman at the well (John 4:24). Though fully personal, God does not live in and through a body as we do, and so is not anchored in a spatiotemporal frame. From this fact, plus the further fact that he is self-existent and not marked as we are by the personal disintegration (lack of concentration and control) that sin has produced in us, several things follow.

First, God is limited neither by space (he is everywhere in his fullness continually) nor by time (there is no "present moment" into which he is locked as we are). Theologians refer to God's freedom from limits and bounds as his infinity, his immensity, and his transcendence. As he upholds everything in being, so he has everything everywhere always before his mind, in its own relation to his all-inclusive plan and purpose for every item and every person in his world.

Second, God is immutable. This means that he is totally consistent: because he is necessarily perfect, he cannot change either for the better or for the worse; and because he is not in time, he is not subject to change as creatures are (2 Peter 3:8). Far from being detached and immobile, he is always active in his world, constantly making new things spring forth (Isaiah 42:9; 2 Corinthians 5:17; Revelation 21:5); but in all this he expresses his perfect character with perfect consistency. It is precisely the immutability of his character that guarantees his adherence to the words he has spoken and the plans he has made (Numbers 23:19; Psalm 33:11; Malachi 3:6; James 1:16-18); and it is this immutability that explains why, when people change their attitude to him, he changes his attitude to them (Genesis 6:5-7; Exodus 32:9-14; 1 Samuel 15:11; Jonah 3:10). The idea that the changelessness of God involves unresponsive indifference to what goes on in his world is the precise opposite of the truth.

Third, God's feelings are not beyond his control, as ours often are. Theologians express this by saying that God is impassible. They mean not that he is impassive and unfeeling but that what he feels, like what he does, is a matter of his own deliberate, voluntary choice and is included in the unity of his infinite being. God is never our victim in the sense that we make him suffer where he had not first chosen to suffer. Scriptures expressing the reality of God's emotions (joy, sorrow, anger, delight, love, hate, etc.) abound, however, and it is a great mistake to forget that God feels—though in a way of necessity that transcends a finite being's experience of emotion.

Fourth, all God's thoughts and actions involve the whole of him. This is his integration, sometimes called his simplicity. It stands in stark contrast to the complexity and lack of integration of our own personal existence, in which, as a result of sin, we are scarcely ever, perhaps never, able to concentrate the whole of our being and all our powers on anything. One aspect of the marvel of God, however, is that he simultaneously gives total and undivided attention not just to one thing at a time but to everything and everyone everywhere in his world past, present, and future (see Matthew 10:29-30).

Fifth, the God who is Spirit must be worshiped in spirit and in truth, as Jesus said (John 4:24). "In spirit" means "from a heart renewed by the Holy Spirit." No rituals, body movements, or devotional formalities constitute worship without involvement of the heart, which the Holy Spirit alone can induce. "In truth" means "on the basis of God's revelation of reality, which culminates in the incarnate Word, Jesus Christ." First and foremost, this is the revelation of what we are as lost sinners and of what God is to us as Creator-Redeemer through Jesus' mediatorial ministry.

No one place on earth is now prescribed as the only center for worship. God's symbolic dwelling in earthly Jerusalem was replaced when the time came (John 4:23) by his dwelling in heavenly Jerusalem, whence Jesus now ministers (Hebrews 12:22-24). In the Spirit, "the Lord is near to all who call on him, to all who call on him in truth," wherever they may be (Psalm 145:18; cf. Hebrews 4:14-16). This worldwide availability of God is part of the good news of the gospel; it is a precious benefit and should not simply be taken for granted.

Concise Theology, pp.28–30

Stand up and bless the Lord,
Ye people of his choice;
Stand up and bless the Lord, your God
With heart and soul and voice.

Though high above all praise,
Above all blessing high,
Who would not fear his holy name,
And praise and magnify?

O for the living flame
From his own altar brought,
To touch our lips, our minds inspire,
And wing to heav'n our thought!

JAMES MONTGOMERY

14

Unchanging:
God's Character and Truth Do Not Change

God is "from all eternity" (Psalm 93:2), "the eternal King" (Jeremiah 10:10), "the immortal God" (Romans 1:23), "who alone is immortal" (1 Timothy 6:16). "Before the mountains were born or you brought forth the earth and the world, from everlasting to everlasting you are God" (Psalm 90:2). Earth and heaven, says the psalmist, "will perish, but you remain; they will all wear out like a garment. Like clothing you will change them and they will be discarded. But *you remain the same,* and your years will never end" (Psalm 102:26-27). "I am the first," says God, "and I am the last" (Isaiah 48:12).

Created things have a beginning and an ending, but not so their Creator. God exists forever, and he is always the same. He does not grow older. His life does not wax or wane. He does not gain new powers nor lose those that he once had. He does not mature or develop. He does not get stronger, or weaker, or wiser, as time goes by. "He cannot change for the better," wrote A.W. Pink, "for he is already perfect; and being perfect, he cannot change for the worse."

God's character does not change. In the course of a human life, tastes and outlook and temper may change radically: a kind, equable person may turn bitter and crotchety; a person of good will may grow cynical and callous. But nothing of this sort happens to the Creator. He never becomes less truthful, or merciful, or just, or good than he used to be. The character of God is today, and always will be, exactly what it was in Bible times.

In Exodus 3, we read how God announced his name to Moses as "I AM WHO I AM" (v. 14)—a phrase of which "Yahweh" (Jehovah, "the Lord") is in effect a shortened form (v. 15). This name is not a description of God, but simply a declaration of his self-existence and his eternal changelessness; a reminder to mankind that he has life in himself, and that what he is now, he is eternally. In Exodus 34, however, we read how God "proclaimed his name, the Lord" to Moses by listing the various facets of his holy character. "The Lord, the Lord [Yahweh], the compassionate and gracious God, slow to anger, abounding in love and faithfulness, maintaining love to thousands, and forgiving wickedness, rebellion and sin. Yet he does not leave the guilty unpunished; he punishes the children and their children" (vv. 5-7).

This proclamation supplements that of Exodus 3 by telling us what in fact Yahweh is; and that of Exodus 3 supplements this by telling us that God is forever what at that moment, three thousand years ago, he told Moses that he was. God's moral character is changeless. So James, in a passage that deals with God's goodness and holiness, his generosity to men and his hostility to sin, speaks of God as one "with whom there is no variation or shadow due to change" (James 1:17, RSV).

God's truth does not change. The words of human beings are unstable things. But not so the words of God. They stand forever, as abidingly valid expressions of his mind and thought. No circumstances prompt him to recall them; no changes in his own thinking require him to amend them. Isaiah writes, "All flesh is grass.... The grass withers.... But the word of our God will stand for ever" (Isaiah 40:6-8, RSV). Similarly, the psalmist says, "Your word, O Lord, is eternal; it stands firm in the heavens. Your faithfulness continues through all generations" (Psalm 119:89-90).

The last verse carries with it the idea of stability. When we read our Bibles, therefore, we need to remember that God still stands behind all the promises, and demands, and statements of purpose, and words of warning, that are there addressed to New Testament believers. These are not relics of a bygone age, but an eternally valid revelation of the mind of God toward his people in all generations.

Knowing God, pp.77–80

ॐ

Great is thy faithfulness, O God my Father,

There is no shadow of turning with thee;

Thou changest not, thy compassions, they fail not:

As thou hast been thou forever will be.

ॐ

THOMAS O. CHISHOLM

15

Unchanging:
God's Ways and Purposes Do Not Change

God continues to act toward sinful men and women in the way that he does in the Bible story. Still he shows his freedom and lordship by discriminating between sinners, causing some to hear the gospel while others do not hear it, and moving some of those who hear it to repentance while leaving others in their unbelief, thus teaching his saints that he owes mercy to none and that it is entirely of his grace, not at all through their own effort, that they themselves have found life.

Still he blesses those on whom he sets his love in a way that humbles them, so that all the glory may be his alone. Still he hates the sins of his people, and uses all kinds of inward and outward pains and griefs to wean their hearts from compromise and disobedience. Still he seeks the fellowship of his people, and sends them both sorrows and joys in order to detach their love from other things and attach it to himself. Still he teaches believers to value his promised gifts by making them wait for those gifts, and compelling them to pray persistently for them, before he bestows them. So we read of God dealing with his people in the Scripture record, and so he deals with them still. His aims and principles of action remain consistent; he does not at any time act out of character. Our ways, we know, are pathetically inconstant—but not God's.

God's purposes never change. "He who is the Glory of Israel does not lie or change his mind," declared Samuel, "for he is not a man, that he should change his mind" (1 Samuel 15:29). Balaam had said the same: "God is not a man, that he should lie, nor a son of man, that he should change his mind. Does he speak and then not act? Does he promise and not fulfill?" (Numbers 23:19).

Repenting means revising one's judgment and changing one's plan of action. God never does this; he never needs to, for his plans are made on the basis of a complete knowledge and control that extend to all things past, present, and future, so that there can be no sudden emergencies or unexpected developments to take him by surprise. God is both omniscient and omnipotent. There is never any need for him to revise his decrees.

What God does in time, he planned from eternity. And all that he planned in eternity he carries out in time. And all that he has in his Word committed himself to do will infallibly be done. Thus we read of "the immutability of his counsel" to bring believers into full enjoyment of their promised inheritance, and of the immutable oath by which he confirmed this counsel to Abraham, the archetypal believer, both for Abraham's own assurance and for ours, too (Hebrews 6:17-18). So it is with all God's announced intentions. They do not change. No part of his eternal plan changes.

Jesus Christ is "the same yesterday and today and forever" (Hebrews 13:8), and his touch has still its ancient power. It still remains true that "he is able to save completely those who come to God through him, because he always lives to intercede for them" (Hebrews 7:25). He never changes. This fact is the strong consolation of all God's people.

Knowing God, pp.79–81

Praise to the living God! All praised be his Name,

Who was, and is, and is to be, for aye the same.

The One Eternal God Ere aught that now appears;

The First, the Last, beyond all thought his timeless years!

Eternal life hath he implanted in the soul;

His love shall be our strength and stay while ages roll.

Praise to the living God! All praised be his name,

Who was, and is, and is to be, for aye the same.

JEWISH DOXOLOGY (MEDIEVAL)
TR. MAX LANDSBERG AND NEWTON MANN

16

Unlimited:
God's Greatness Has No Bounds

How may we form a right idea of God's greatness? The Bible teaches us two steps that we must take. The first is to *remove from our thoughts of God limits that would make him small.* The second is to *compare him with powers and forces that we regard as great.*

For an example of what the first step involves, look at Psalm 139, where the psalmist meditates on the infinite and unlimited nature of God's presence, and knowledge, and power, in relation to people. We are always in God's presence, he says. You can cut yourself off from your fellow human beings, but you cannot get away from your Creator. "You hem me in—behind and before.... Where can I go from your Spirit? Where can I flee from your presence? If I go up to the heavens [the sky], you are there; if I make my bed in the depths [the underworld], you are there. If I rise on the wings of the dawn, if I settle on the far side of the sea," I still cannot escape from the presence of God: "even there your hand will guide me" (vv. 5-10). Nor can darkness, which hides me from human sight, shield me from God's gaze (vv. 11-12).

And just as there are no bounds to his presence with me, so there are no limits to his knowledge of me. Just as I am never left alone, so I never go unnoticed. "O Lord, you have searched me and you know me. You know when I sit and when I rise [all my actions and movements]; you perceive my thoughts [all that goes on in my mind] from afar.... You are familiar with all my ways [all my habits, plans, aims, desires, as well as all my life to date]. Before a word is on my tongue [spoken, or meditated] you know it completely, O Lord" (vv. 1-4).

I can hide my heart, and my past, and my future plans, from those around me, but I cannot hide anything from God. I can talk in a way that deceives my fellow creatures as to what I really am, but nothing I say or do can deceive God. He sees through all my reserve and pretense; he knows me as I really am, better indeed than I know myself.

A God whose presence and scrutiny I could evade would be a small and trivial deity. But the true God is great and terrible, just because he is always with me and his eye is always upon me. Living becomes an awesome business when you realize that you spend every moment of your life in the sight and company of an omniscient, omnipresent Creator.

Nor is this all. The all-seeing God is also God almighty, the resources of whose power are already revealed to me by the amazing complexity of my own physical body, which he made for me. Confronted with this, the psalmist's meditations turn to worship. "I praise you because I am fearfully and wonderfully made; your works are wonderful" (v. 14).

Here, then, is the first step in apprehending the greatness of God: to realize how unlimited are his wisdom, and his presence, and his power. Look at Job 37–41, the chapters in which God himself takes up Elihu's recognition that "with God is terrible majesty" (37:22, KJV), and sets before Job a tremendous display of his wisdom and power in nature, and asks Job if he can match such "majesty" as this (40:9-11), and convinces him that, since he cannot, he should not presume to find fault with God's handling of Job's own case, which also goes far beyond Job's understanding.

Knowing God, pp.85–86

Lord, thou hast searched me and dost know
Where'er I rest, where'er I go;
Thou knowest all that I have planned,
And all my ways are in thy hand.

My words from thee I cannot hide;
I feel thy power on every side;
O wondrous knowledge, awful might,
Unfathomed depth, unmeasured height!

Where can I go apart from thee,
Or whither from thy presence flee?
In heaven? It is thy dwelling fair;
In death's abode? Lo, thou art there.

If I the wings of morning take,
And far away my dwelling make,
The hand that leadeth me is thine,
And my support thy power divine.

BASED ON PSALM 139
"THE PSALTER HYMNAL," 1927

17

Incomparability:
No One Can Rival God

Look at Isaiah 40. Here God speaks to people whose mood is the mood of many Christians today—despondent people, cowed people, secretly despairing people; people against whom the tide of events has been running for a very long time; people who have ceased to believe that the cause of Christ can ever prosper again. Now see how God through his prophet reasons with them.

Look at the *tasks* I have done, he says. Could you do them? Could any man do them? "Who has measured the waters in the hollow of his hand, or with the breadth of his hand marked off the heavens? Who has held the dust of the earth in a basket, or weighed the mountains on the scales and the hills in a balance?" (v. 12). Are you wise enough, and mighty enough, to do things like that? But I am, or I could not have made this world at all. Behold your God!

Look now at the *nations,* the prophet continues: the great national powers, at whose mercy you feel yourselves to be. Assyria, Egypt, Babylon—you stand in awe of them, and feel afraid of them, so vastly do their armies and resources exceed yours. But now consider how God stands related to those mighty forces that you fear so much. "Surely the nations are like a drop in a bucket; they are regarded as dust on the scales; ... Before him all the nations are as nothing; they are regarded by him as worthless and less than nothing" (vv. 15, 17). You tremble before the nations, because you are much weaker than they; but God is so much greater than the nations that they are as nothing to him. Behold your God!

Look next at the *world*. Consider the size of it, the variety and complexity of it; think of the more than five thousand millions who populate it and of the vast sky above it. What puny figures you and I are, by comparison with the whole planet on which we live! Yet what is this entire mighty planet by comparison with God? "He sits enthroned above the circle of the earth, and its people are like grasshoppers. He stretches out the heavens like a canopy, and spreads them out like a tent to live in" (Isaiah 40:22). The world dwarfs us all, but God dwarfs the world. The world is his footstool, above which he sits secure. He is greater than the world and all that is in it, so that all the feverish activity of its bustling millions does no more to affect him than the chirping and jumping of grasshoppers in the summer sun does to affect us. Behold your God!

Look, fourthly, at the world's *great ones*—the governors whose laws and policies determine the welfare of millions; the would-be world rulers, the dictators and empire builders, who have it in their power to plunge the globe into war. Think of Sennacherib and Nebuchadnezzar; think of Alexander, Napoleon, Hitler. Think, today, of the president of the USA and leaders around the world. Do you suppose that it is really these top men who determine which way the world shall go? Think again, for God is greater than the world's great men. Behold your God!

Let Isaiah now apply to us the Bible doctrine of the majesty of God by asking us the three questions that he here puts in God's name to disillusioned and downcast Israelites.

"'To whom then will you compare me, that I should be like him?' says the Holy One" (Isaiah 40:25, RSV). This question rebukes *wrong thoughts about God*. This is where most of us go astray. Our thoughts of God are not great enough; we fail to reckon with the reality of his limitless wisdom and power. Because we ourselves are limited and weak, we imagine that at some points God is too, and find it hard to believe that he is not. We think of God as too much like what we are. Put this mistake right, says God; learn to acknowledge the full majesty of your incomparable God and Savior.

"Why sayest thou, O Jacob, and speakest, O Israel, My way is hid from the Lord and my judgment is passed over from my God?" (Isaiah 40:27, KJV). This question rebukes *wrong thoughts about ourselves*. God has not abandoned us any more than he abandoned Job. He never abandons anyone on whom he has set his love; nor does Christ, the good shepherd, ever lose track of his sheep. It is as false as it is irreverent to accuse God of forgetting, or overlooking, or losing interest in, the state and needs of his own people. If you have been resigning yourself to the thought that God has left you high and dry, seek grace to be ashamed of yourself. Such unbelieving pessimism deeply dishonors our great God and Savior.

"Hast thou not known? hast thou not heard, that the everlasting God, the Lord, the Creator of the ends of the earth, fainteth not, neither is weary?" (Isaiah 40:28, KJV). This question rebukes *our slowness to believe in God's majesty*. God would shame us out of our unbelief. "What is the trouble?" he asks. "Have you been imagining that I, the Creator, have grown old and tired? Has nobody ever told you the truth about me?"

The rebuke is well deserved by many of us. How slow we are to believe in God *as God*, sovereign, all-seeing, and almighty! How little we make of the majesty of our Lord and Savior Christ! The need for us is to "wait upon the Lord" in meditations on his majesty, till we find our strength renewed through the writing of these things upon our hearts.

Knowing God, pp.86–89

❧

Lord, with joy my heart expands

Before the wonders of thy hands;

Great works, Jehovah, thou hast wrought,

Exceeding deep thine ev'ry thought;

A foolish man know not their worth,

Nor he whose mind is of the earth.

When as the grass the wicked grow,

When sinners flourish here below,

Then is their endless ruin nigh,

But thou, O Lord, art throned on high;

Thy foes shall fall before thy might,

The wicked shall be put to flight.

❧

PSALM 92:1-9, 12-15
THE PSALTER, 1912

18

Majesty:
God's Greatness Is Splendid

Our word *majesty* comes from the Latin; it means *greatness*. When we ascribe majesty to someone, we are acknowledging greatness in that person and voicing our respect for it: as, for instance, when we speak of "Her Majesty" the Queen.

Now, *majesty* is a word that the Bible uses to express the thought of the greatness of God, our Maker and our Lord. "The Lord reigns, he is robed in *majesty*.... Your throne was established long ago" (Psalm 93:1-2). "They will speak of the glorious splendor of your *majesty*, and I will meditate on your wonderful works" (Psalm 145:5). Peter, recalling his vision of Christ's royal glory at the transfiguration, says, "We were eyewitnesses of his *majesty*" (2 Peter 1:16).

In Hebrews, the phrase *the majesty* twice does duty for *God*; Christ, we are told, at his ascension sat down "at the right hand of *the Majesty* in heaven," "at the right hand of the throne of *the Majesty* in heaven" (Hebrews 1:3; 8:1). The word *majesty*, when applied to God, is always a declaration of his greatness and an invitation to worship. The same is true when the Bible speaks of God as being *on high* and *in heaven*; the thought here is not that God is far distant from us in space, but that he is far above us in greatness, and therefore is to be adored. "Great is the Lord, and most worthy of praise" (Psalm 48:1). "For the Lord is the great God, the great King.... Come, let us bow down in worship" (Psalm 95:3, 6). The Christian's instincts of trust and worship are stimulated very powerfully by knowledge of the greatness of God.

Right at the start of the Bible story, through the wisdom of divine inspiration, the narrative is told in such a way to impress upon the twin truths that the God to whom we are being introduced is both *personal* and *majestic*.

Nowhere in the Bible is the personal nature of God expressed in more vivid terms. He deliberates with himself, "Let us ..." (Genesis 1:26). He brings the animals to Adam to see what Adam will call them (2:19). He walks in the garden, calling to Adam (3:8-9). He asks people questions (3:11-13; 4:9; 16:8). He comes down from heaven in order to find out what his creatures are doing (11:5; 18:20-33). He is so grieved by human wickedness that he repents of making them (6:6-7).

Representations of God like these are meant to bring home to us the fact that the God with whom we have to do is not a mere cosmic principle, impersonal and indifferent, but a living Person, thinking, feeling, active, approving of good, disapproving of evil, interested in his creatures all the time.

But we are not to gather from these passages that God's knowledge and power are limited, or that he is normally absent and so unaware of what is going on in the world except when he comes specially to investigate. These same chapters rule out all such ideas by setting before us a presentation of God's greatness no less vivid than that of his personality.

The God of Genesis is the Creator, bringing order out of chaos, calling life into being by his word, making Adam from earth's dust and Eve from Adam's rib (chaps. 1–2). And he is Lord of all that he has made. He curses the ground and subjects mankind to physical death, thus changing his original perfect world order (3:17–24); he floods the earth in judgment, destroying all life except that in the ark (chaps. 6–8); he confounds human language and scatters the builders of Babel (11:7-9); he overthrows Sodom and Gomorrah by (apparently) a volcanic eruption (19:24-25). Abraham truly calls him "the Judge of all the earth" (18:25), and rightly adopts Melchizedek's name for him, "God Most High, maker of heaven and earth" (14:19-22, RSV). He is present everywhere, and he observes everything: Cain's murder (4:9), mankind's corruption (6:5), Hagar's destitution (16:7). Well did Hagar name him *El Roi*, "the God who sees me," and call her son Ishmael, "God hears," for God does in truth both hear and see, and nothing escapes him.

His own name for himself is *El Shaddai*, "God Almighty," and all his actions illustrate the omnipotence that this name proclaims. He promises Abraham and his wife a son in their nineties, and he rebukes Sarah for her incredulous—and, as it proved, unjustified—laughter: "Is anything too hard for the Lord?" (18:14). And it is not only at isolated moments that God takes control of events, either; all history is under his sway. Proof of this is given by his detailed predictions of the tremendous destiny that he purposed to work out for Abraham's seed (12:1-3; 13:14-17; 15:13-21; and so on).

Such, in brief, is the majesty of God, according to the first chapters of Genesis.

Knowing God, pp.82–85

～

Loud hallelujahs to Thy name
Angels and seraphim proclaim:
The heavens and all the powers on high
With rapture constantly do cry.

"O holy, holy, holy Lord!
Thou God of hosts, by all adored;
Earth and the heavens are full of thee,
Thy light, thy power, thy majesty."

Glory to thee, O God most high!
Father, we praise thy majesty,
The Son, the Spirit, we adore:
One Godhead, blest for evermore.

～

GELL'S COLLECTION, 1815

19

Glory: Praise God for His Glorious Grace

In the New Testament, the word "glory" carries two interlocked layers of meaning, each of which entails the other. Layer one is the manifested praiseworthiness of the Creator; layer two is the praise that this draws from his creatures. Which layer is "on top" depends on whether the reference is to the glory that God *has and shows and gives* or to that that he *is given*. For we in gratitude bless the God who in grace has blessed us, and this is to glorify the One who is even now glorifying us by remaking us in Christ's image (see 2 Corinthians 3:18 and Ephesians 1:3).

In the Old Testament, God displayed his glory in typical, visual form as an awe-inspiring expanse of bright light (the *shekinah*, as later Judaism called it). This was the sign of his beneficent presence in both the tabernacle and the temple (Exodus 40:34; 1 Kings 8:10ff.). The essential and abiding revelation of God's glory, however, was given by his great acts of merited judgment and unmerited love.

So, when the Word was made flesh in lowliness, having emptied himself of the glory he shared with the Father before creation, the breathtaking brilliance of the *shekinah* was hidden, save for the one isolated moment of transfiguration; yet Jesus' disciples could testify, "we beheld his glory," the glory of personal deity "full of grace and truth" (John 1:14; cf. 17:5; Philippians 2:7, RSV). Great as is the physical glory of *shekinah* light, the moral glory of God's redeeming love is greater. Those today whom God enlightens to understand the gospel never see the *shekinah*, but they behold the glory of God in the face of Jesus Christ (2 Corinthians 4:6).

When in the traditional Lord's Prayer doxology we ascribe the glory, along with the royal rule, to God forever, we are, first, telling God (and thus reminding ourselves) that he, our Maker and Redeemer, is, and always will be, glorious in all he does, especially in his acts of grace ("we give thanks to thee *for thy great glory*"); and, second, we are committing ourselves, now and always, to worship and adore him for it all ("*glory be* to God on high"). The doxology thus makes the Lord's Prayer end in praise, just as the Christian life itself will do: for while petition will cease with this life, the happy task of giving God glory will last for all eternity.

Now let us test our spiritual quality.

The principle of human sin (which is the devil's image in man) is this: glory is not God's, but mine. Accordingly, we parade what we think of as our glory, so that admiring watchers will give us glory. This is one facet of our pride: we call it vanity. Vain persons put on a show with their features, physical shape, clothes, skills, position, influence, homes, brains, acquaintanceships, or whatever they are most proud of, expect applause, and feel resentful and hurt if people do not play up to them and act impressed.

But Christians know that vanity is a lie, for it assumes that it is we who should be praised and admired for what we are; and that is not so. Christianity teaches us, not indeed to pretend that we lack qualities which we know very well that we have, but to acknowledge that all we have is God's gift to us, so that he should be praised and admired for it rather than we.

The test is to ask yourself how pleased, or how displeased, you become if God is praised while you are not, and equally if you are praised while God is not. The mature Christian is content not to have glory given to him, but it troubles him if men are not glorifying God. It pained the dying Puritan, Richard Baxter, the outstanding devotional writer of his day, when visitors praised him for his books. "I was but a pen in God's hand," he whispered, "and what praise is due to a pen?" That shows the mentality of the mature; they want to cry every moment, "Give glory to God!—for it is his due, and his alone!"

Growing in Christ, pp.211–12

៩

To God on high all glory be,
And thanks, that he's so gracious,
That hence to all eternity,
No evil shall oppress us:
His word declares good will to men,
On earth is peace restored again,
Through Jesus Christ our Savior.

We humbly thee adore, and praise,
And laud for thy great glory;
Father, thy kingdom lasts always,
Not frail, nor transitory:
Thy power is endless as thy praise,
Thou speak'st, the universe obeys:
In such a Lord we're happy.

៩

NIKOLAUS DECIUS

20

Mystery:
God Is Greater Than We Can Ever Grasp

God is great, says Scripture, greater than we can grasp. Theology states this by describing him as incomprehensible—not in the sense that logic is somehow different for him than it is for us, so that we cannot follow the workings of his mind at all, but in the sense that we can never understand him fully, just because he is infinite and we are finite. Scripture pictures God as dwelling not only in thick and impenetrable darkness but also in unapproachable light (Psalm 97:2; 1 Timothy 6:16), and both images express the same thought: our Creator is above us, and it is beyond our power to take his measure in any way.

This is sometimes expressed by speaking of the mystery of God, using that word not in the biblical sense of a secret that God has now revealed (Daniel 2:29-30; Ephesians 3:2-6), but in the more recently developed sense of a reality that we lack the capacity to understand properly, no matter how much is said about it. God tells us in the Bible that creation, providential government, the Trinity, the Incarnation, the regenerating work of the Spirit, union with Christ in his death and resurrection, and the inspiration of Scripture—to go no further—are facts, and we take his word for it that they are; but we believe that they are without knowing how they can be. As creatures, we are unable fully to comprehend either the being or the actions of the Creator.

As it would be wrong, however, to suppose ourselves to know everything about God (and so in effect to imprison him in the box of our own limited notion of him), so it would be wrong to doubt whether our concept constitutes real knowledge of him. Part of the significance of our creation in God's image is that we are able both to know about him and to know him relationally in a true if limited sense of "know"; and what God tells us in Scripture about himself is true as far as it goes. Calvin spoke of God as having condescended to our weakness and accommodated himself to our capacity, both in the inspiring of the Scriptures and in the incarnating of the Son, so that he might give us genuine understanding of himself. The form and substance of a parent's baby talk bears no comparison with the full contents of that parent's mind, which he or she could express in full if talking to another adult; but the child receives from the baby talk factual information, real if limited, about the parent, and responsive love and trust grow accordingly. That is the analogy here.

Now we see why our Creator presents himself to us anthropomorphically, as having a face (Exodus 33:11), a hand (1 Samuel 5:11), an arm (Isaiah 53:1), ears (Nehemiah 1:6), eyes (Job 28:10), and feet (Nahum 1:3), and as sitting on a throne (1 Kings 22:19), flying on the wind (Psalm 18:10), and fighting in battle (2 Chronicles 32:8; Isaiah 63:1-6). These are not descriptions of what God is in himself but of what he is to us: namely, the transcendent Lord who relates to his people as Father and friend, and acts as their ally. God sets himself before us in this way to draw us out in worship, love, and trust, even though conceptually we are always like the young children who hear their parents' baby talk and know the talker only in part (1 Corinthians 13:12).

We should never forget that in any case theology is for doxology: the truest expression of trust in a great God will always be worship, and it will always be proper worship to praise God for being far greater than we can know.

Concise Theology, pp.51–53

God moves in a mysterious way
His wonders to perform:
He plants his footsteps in the sea,
And rides upon the storm.

Ye fearful saints, fresh courage take;
The clouds ye so much dread
Are big with mercy, and shall break
In blessings on your head.

Judge not the Lord by feeble sense,
But trust him for his grace;
Behind a frowning providence
He hides a smiling face.

Blind unbelief is sure to err,
And scan his work in vain;
God is his own interpreter,
And he will make it plain.

WILLIAM COWPER

21

Promise-Maker:
God Never Breaks His Word

God has made his purpose a matter of promise to us. The Bible is full of particular promises in which aspects of that purpose are spelled out as a basis for our responsive trust. Were it not so, you could hardly call our contact with God a personal relationship at all. Real personal relationships always involve personal commitments, and promises are the utterances that regulate such commitments. A promise is a word that reaches into the future, creating a bond of obligation on the part of the one who gives it and of expectation on the part of the one who receives it. In this sense it is what logicians call a "performative" word, one that brings about a new state of affairs for those by whom and to whom it is spoken. That our mighty Creator should have bound himself to use his power fulfilling promises to us—"very great and precious promises," as 2 Peter 1:4 puts it—is one of the wonders of biblical religion.

All God's promises relate, one way or another, to his purpose of glorifying himself by blessing his human creatures. There are announcements of his purpose of:

- preserving earth's natural order for humanity until history ends (Genesis 9:8-17);

- maintaining an abiding covenant relationship with Abraham and his descendants, including all who are in Christ (Genesis 17:1-8; Galatians 3:7-9, 14, 22-29);

- bestowing particular benefits on his people here and now according to their needs—forgiving their sins, delivering them from evils, strengthening them in their weaknesses, comforting them in their sorrows, guiding them in their perplexities, and so on;

- sending Christ back to this world in glory, to create new heavens and a new earth, and to bring his people into a final state of joy with their Savior compared with which, as C.S. Lewis says somewhere, "the highest raptures of earthly lovers will appear as mere milk and water."

All God's universal promises to his people relate to the fulfilling of his saving purpose for them. He wants us to see this and be glad of it.

Scripture also tells of God giving and miraculously fulfilling many specific promises to many special people—promises of progeny to particular childless wives, for instance (Genesis 17:15-19; 18:10-15; 30:22; Judges 13; 1 Samuel 1:9-20; Luke 1:7-20), and to the Virgin Mary (Luke 1:26-38). We need to be careful in the lessons we draw from such stories. Because these miraculously born children each had a special role in the fulfilling of God's purpose for the world, we must not read these narratives as constituting a divine promise of pregnancy to all childless wives who pray.

Nor, to give another example, may we treat narratives of Jesus' miraculous healings in Palestine, where he evidenced his messianic claims (see Matthew 11:2-6), as constituting a promise of similar healing to any and all who pray for it today.

Nonetheless, all biblical stories of specific promises fulfilled by God's power, and of particular gracious displays of that power in blessing, remind us of what God can do. They encourage us to rely on his omnipotence and trust him to fulfill his purpose in each Christian's life in the way he sees best.

Rediscovering Holiness, pp.228–30

〜

How firm a foundation, ye saints of the Lord,

Is laid for your faith in his excellent word!

What more can he say than to you he hath said,

To you who for refuge to Jesus have fled.

"Fear not, I am with thee, O be not dismayed,

For I am thy God, and will still give thee aid;

I'll strengthen thee, help thee, and cause thee to stand,

Upheld by my righteous, omnipotent hand."

〜

"K" IN JOHN RIPPON'S "SELECTION OF HYMNS," 1787

22

Energy:
God Can Do More Than We Ask or Imagine

Most modern talk of power has to do with impersonal forces in nature or society, or human prerogatives of control, but our present theme is not either of these. We are talking about the divine energy that brought the universe into existence when nothing but God himself was in existence; the energy that upholds the universe in being every moment (for no created thing is self-sustaining), and that orders, controls, and directs everything that happens within the universe at any time. Our immediate concern is with the operation of this energy in the vast complexity of our human lives—both in the intricacies of our bodily functions and in the greater intricacies of our conscious personal being. These intricacies include our thinking, planning, decision making, and maintaining of commitments; our habits and behavior patterns; our actions and reactions; our use of our skills, natural and acquired, and of our creativity; our hopes, fears, joys, pains, and what they do to us; our relational, moral, and aesthetic experiences; all our ups and downs of feeling, from exuberance to exhaustion, from ecstasy to apathy, and from delight to depression; and so on. All these facets of our life are touched by the energy of God.

Most particularly, we are focusing on God's exercise of his energy in redemptive grace. By this he regenerates, assures, sanctifies, alters our disposition, changes our character through moving us to practice Christlike virtues, equips us to serve others, and enables us to do and be for God what, left to ourselves, we never could have been or have done. The power here is not the sort of power that we humans can grab hold of and manipulate. It is power that belongs to God, and that he alone manages. Just as my will is me in action, so God's power is God in action. When God acts upon human beings, they are under his control, but he is not under theirs. God's power is sovereign power, sovereignly employed.

As God exerted great power in creation, and exerts great power in his providential upholding and shaping of things, so he has committed himself to exert great power in the saving and upbuilding of his people. In Ephesians 3:10, Paul, having declared that the riches of Christ are unsearchable, explains the divine intent in the economy of grace as "that now, through the church, the manifold wisdom of God should be made known to the rulers and authorities in the heavenly realms."

The vivid picture that these words conjure up is one of the church as God's display area, where he shows an audience of watching angels what a breathtaking variety of wonderful things he can do in and through sin-damaged human beings. My three Greek dictionaries render the Greek word translated "manifold" as much-variegated, very many-sided, and of greatly differing colors—which renderings give us some idea of the range and resourcefulness of God's ongoing work of power in the church. The church as a multiracial, multicultural community is like a beautiful tapestry. Yes—and also as a multirepair shop, where disordered and broken-down lives, made ugly by sin, are being reconstructed in Christlike shape. The wisdom of God that Paul has in view is not just the wisdom that brings Jew and Gentile together in the body of Christ, but is also the wisdom that directs the power that quickens the spiritually dead and makes new creatures of them in a new and lovely fellowship of holiness and love (Ephesians 2:1-10, cf. 4:20-24).

Great is the power of God in the lives of the people of God!

Paul's stupendous prayer that follows, asking God that his readers might be empowered to know the full dimensions of the love of Christ so that they might be filled to all the fullness of God, and his great doxology after that, celebrating the fact that God can do "immeasurably more than all we ask or imagine" (Ephesians 3:20), further confirm the point. The potential of God's power in our lives is incalculable. Do we reckon with this fact?

Rediscovering Holiness, pp.223–25

When through the deep waters I call thee to go,
The rivers of sorrow shall not thee o'erflow;
For I will be near thee, thy troubles to bless,
And sanctify to thee thy deepest distress.

When through fiery trials thy pathway shall lie,
My grace, all sufficient, shall be thy supply.
The flame shall not hurt thee; I only design
Thy dross to consume, and thy gold to refine.

"K" IN JOHN RIPPON'S "SELECTION OF HYMNS," 1787

23

Wisdom:
God Knows What Is Best

Wisdom in Scripture means choosing the best and noblest end at which to aim, along with the most appropriate and effective means to it. Human wisdom is displayed in the Old Testament Wisdom books (Job, Psalms, Proverbs, Ecclesiastes, and Song of Songs, showing how to suffer, pray, live, enjoy, and love, respectively) and in James' letter (enforcing consistent Christian behavior): it means making the "fear" of God—that is, reverent worship and service of him—one's goal (Proverbs 1:7; 9:10; Ecclesiastes 12:13) and cultivating prudence, fortitude, forbearance, and zeal as means to it. God's wisdom is seen in his works of creation, preservation, and redemption: it is his choice of his own glory as his goal (Psalm 46:10; Isaiah 42:8; 48:11), and his decision to achieve it first by creating a marvelous variety of things and people (Psalm 104:24; Proverbs 3:19-20), second by kindly providences of all sorts (Psalm 145:13-16; Acts 14:17), and third by the redemptive "wisdom" of "Christ crucified" (1 Corinthians 1:18-2:16) and the resultant world church (Ephesians 3:10).

The outworking of God's wisdom involves the expression of his will in both senses that that phrase bears. In the first and fundamental sense, God's will is his decision, or decree, about what shall happen—"his eternal purpose, according to the counsel of his will, whereby, for his own glory, he hath foreordained whatsoever comes to pass" (Westminster Shorter Catechism Q.7). This is God's will of events, referred to in Ephesians 1:11. In the second and secondary sense, the will of God is his command, that is, his instruction, given in Scripture, as to how people should and should not behave: it is sometimes called his will of precept (see Romans 12:2; Ephesians 5:17; Colossians 1:9; 1 Thessalonians 4:3-6). Some of its requirements are rooted in his holy character, which we are to imitate: such are the principles of the Decalogue and the two great commandments (Exodus 20:1-17; Matthew 22:37-40; cf. Ephesians 4:32-5:2). Some of its requirements spring simply from the divine institution: such were circumcision and the Old Testament sacrificial and purity laws, and such are baptism and the Lord's Supper today. But all bind the conscience alike, and God's plan of events already includes the "good works" of obedience that those who believe will perform (Ephesians 2:10).

It is sometimes hard to believe that costly obedience, putting us at a disadvantage in the world (as loyal obedience to God often does), is part of a predestined plan for furthering both God's glory and our own good (Romans 8:28). But we are to glorify God by believing that it is so, and that one day we shall see it to be so; for his wisdom is supreme and never fails. Making known his will of precept, and governing the responses of human free agency to it, is one means whereby God accomplishes his will of events, even when the response is one of unbelief and disobedience. Paul illustrates this when he tells the Romans that Israel's unbelief has its place in God's plan for advancing the gospel (Romans 11:11-15, 25-32): a realization that prompts the cry: "Oh, the depth of the riches of the wisdom ... of God! ... To him be the glory forever! Amen" (vv. 33, 36). Let that be our cry, too.

Concise Theology, pp.48–50

Awake, my tongue, thy tribute bring
To him who gave thee pow'r to sing;
Praise him who is all praise above,
The source of wisdom and of love.

How vast his knowledge, how profound
A deep where all our thoughts are drowned:
The stars he numbers, and their names
He gives to all those heav'nly flames.

Thro' each bright world above, behold!
Ten thousand thousand charms unfold;
Earth, air, and mighty seas combine
To speak his wisdom all divine.

But in redemption, O what grace!
Its wonders, O what thought can trace!
Here, wisdom shines forever bright;
Praise him, my soul, with sweet delight.

JOHN NEEDHAM

24

Perfectly Reliable:
God Is Our Source, Our Stay, and Our End

God has shown himself to be a *personal* being, one who calls himself "I" and speaks to humans as "you." When, before the Exodus, he spoke to Moses at the burning bush, he gave his name as "I AM WHO I AM." This name, like other God-given names (Abraham, Israel, Jesus, etc.), was a source of information about its bearer: it declared, on the one hand, God's transcendent personality, his freedom and purposefulness, and on the other hand, his self-sufficiency and omnipotence. The name "Yahweh" is a standing witness against any notion of God as a mere impersonal principle: it declares that back of everything stands, not an aimless force—blind fate, or chance—but an almighty Person with a mind and will of his own.

When God brought his work of revelation to its climax by sending into the world his Son and his Spirit, he thereby showed himself to be tri-personal—three Persons in one God. The Trinity is at the heart of the Christian revelation. "Father, Son, and Holy Spirit" is God's New Testament "name."

God has shown himself a *moral* being, One supremely concerned about right and wrong, whose dealings with human beings must be understood in moral terms, since they are determined by moral considerations. When at Sinai Moses asked to see God's glory, God proclaimed before him the following exposition of his "name": "The Lord, the Lord [Yahweh], the compassionate and gracious God, slow to anger, abounding in love and faithfulness, maintaining love to thousands, and forgiving wickedness, rebellion and sin. Yet he does not leave the guilty unpunished; he punishes the children and their children for the sin of the fathers..." (Exodus 34:6f.). God is perfect, not only in power, but also in love and purity, a God "of infinite power, wisdom, and goodness," "a Spirit, infinite, eternal and unchangeable, in His being, wisdom, power, holiness, justice, goodness, and truth" (Westminster Shorter Catechism). God's own exposition of his name rules out all thought of him as capricious, inconstant, untrustworthy, or unloving.

God has revealed himself to be the *source, stay, and end* of all creation, and of mankind in particular. "For from him and through him and to him are all things" (Romans 11:36). Paul develops these foundation-truths of theism in his sermon to the Athenian idolaters about the "unknown God" (Acts 17:22ff.). First, he speaks of God as our *source*, the One who brought us into existence. "The God who made the world and everything in it" (v. 24) "from one man ... made every nation of men, that they should inhabit the whole earth" (v. 26). Then Paul speaks of God as our *stay*, the One who "gives all men life and breath and everything else," so that "in him we live and move and have our being" (v. 25, 28). We depend upon God every moment for our existence: creatures only remain in being through the constant exercise of His upholding power (cf. Hebrews 1:3). He, God transcendent, above and beyond and apart from his world, and entirely independent of it (cf. Acts 17:24f.), is also God immanent, in the world as the One who is over it, permeating and upholding it as the One who orders its goings and controls its course. Lastly, Paul speaks of God as our *end*. God made men, he says, "so that men would seek him" (v. 27). Man exists for God, and godlessness is a denial of man's own nature. Humanity is only perfected in those who know God. "Man's chief end is to glorify God, and to enjoy him forever" *(Westminster Shorter Catechism).*

This God, Paul adds, "is not far from each one of us" (v. 27). Though he is "Lord of heaven and earth" (v. 24), infinitely great, he is not remote. Just the opposite is true. The God who made the world is always, inescapably, our environment. Omniscient, omnipresent, unsleeping, undistracted, he is before and behind us, ever taking knowledge of us, whether or not we acknowledge him.

God Has Spoken, pp.47–50

I sing the mighty power of God,
that made the mountains rise,
that spread the flowing seas abroad
and built the lofty skies.
I sing the wisdom that ordained the sun to rule the day;
the moon shines full at his command, and all the stars obey.

I sing the goodness of the Lord,
that filled the earth with food;
he formed the creatures with his Word,
and then pronounced them good.
Lord, how thy wonders are displayed,
where'er I turn my eye.
If I survey the ground I tread,
or gaze upon the sky!

There's not a plant or flower below,
but makes thy glories known;
and clouds arise, and tempests blow,
by order from thy throne;
while all that borrows life from thee is ever in thy care,
and everywhere that I could be, thou, God, art present there.

ᘰ

ISAAC WATTS

- 25 -

Loving Affection:
God Longs for Our Friendship

Why has God spoken? He is self-sufficient and does not need men's gifts or service (Acts 17:25); to what end, then, does he bother to speak to us?

The truly staggering answer that the Bible gives to this question is that God's purpose in revelation is to *make friends* with us. It was to this end that he created us rational beings, bearing his image, able to think and hear and speak and love; he wanted there to be genuine personal affection and friendship, two-sided, between himself and us—a relation, not like that between a man and his dog, but like that of a father to his child, or a husband to his wife. Loving friendship between two persons has no ulterior motive; it is an end in itself. And this is God's end in revelation. He speaks to us simply to fulfill the purpose for which we were made; that is, to bring into being a relationship in which he is a friend to us, and we to him, he finding his joy in giving us gifts and we finding ours in giving him thanks.

That God made man to be his friend appears from the third chapter of Genesis, where we find God walking in the garden in the cool of the day, looking for Adam to join him and share his company (Genesis 3:8). That, despite sin, God still wants human friends appears from Christ's statement that God seeks true worshipers (John 4:23); for *worship*, the acknowledging of *worth*, is an activity of friendship at its highest (hence 'with my body I thee *worship*' in the marriage service). God wants men and women to know the joy of the love-relationship from which worship springs, and of the worship itself in which that relationship finds its happiest expression. The supreme example of such a relationship with God is that of Abraham, who worshiped God and trusted and obeyed his word even to the point of being willing to surrender his son for sacrifice— and Abraham, we are told, "was called *God's friend*" (James 2:23, alluding to Isaiah 41:8; cf. 2 Chronicles 20:7). It is to make us his friends, as Abraham was, that God has spoken to us.

And if he was to succeed in making friends, it was absolutely necessary that he should speak to us; for the only way to make friends with a person is by talking to him and getting him to talk back to you. Friendship without conversation is a contradiction in terms. A man with whom I never speak will never be my friend. The thing is impossible.

Friendship is never fully enjoyed while the friends are out of each other's sight. Looks express affection better than mere words can, and the delight of a love-relationship can only be complete when we are looking into the beloved one's face. So, when someone we are fond of is away from us, we write, "I'm longing to *see* you again." The Bible looks on to a day when the relationship between God and his human friends will be made perfect in this way, a day when, in addition to hearing his voice, they will see his face. "Now we see but a poor reflection as in a mirror; then we shall see *face to face*" (1 Corinthians 13:12). Similarly, Scripture tells us that in the New Jerusalem those whom Jesus called "friends" when he was on earth (see John 15:13-15) "will *see his face*" (Revelation 22:4). Thus, dying Mr. Stand-fast, in Bunyan's *Pilgrim's Progress*, could confidently declare: "I am going now to see that Head that was crowned with thorns, and that Face that was spit upon, for me. I have formerly lived by hearsay, and faith, but now I go where I shall live by sight, and shall be with him, in whose company I delight myself."

And by this vision both friendship and revelation will be perfected. But meanwhile God's friendship with men and women begins and grows through speech: his to us in revelation, and ours to him in prayer and praise. Though I cannot see God, he and I can yet be personal friends, because in revelation he talks to me.

God Has Spoken, pp.50–52

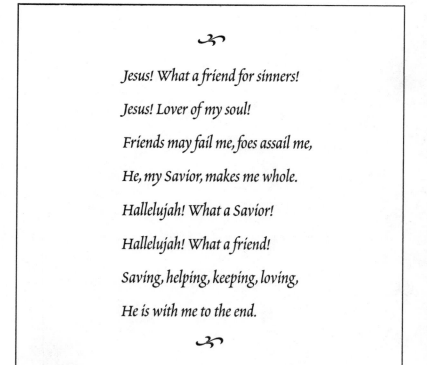

Jesus! What a friend for sinners!

Jesus! Lover of my soul!

Friends may fail me, foes assail me,

He, my Savior, makes me whole.

Hallelujah! What a Savior!

Hallelujah! What a friend!

Saving, helping, keeping, loving,

He is with me to the end.

J. WILBUR CHAPMAN

Holiness:
God the Judge Justifies Sinners

When Scripture calls God, or individual persons of the Godhead, "holy" the word signifies everything about God that sets him apart from us and makes him an object of awe, adoration, and dread to us. It covers all aspects of his transcendent greatness and moral perfection and thus is an attribute of all his attributes, pointing to the "Godness" of God at every point. Every facet of God's nature and every aspect of his character may properly be spoken of as holy, just because it is his. The core of the concept, however, is God's purity, which cannot tolerate any form of sin (Habakkuk 1:13) and thus calls sinners to constant self-abasement in his presence (Isaiah 6:5).

Justice, which means doing in all circumstances things that are right, is one expression of God's holiness. God displays his justice as legislator and judge and also as promise-keeper and pardoner of sin. His moral law, requiring behavior that matches his own, is "holy, righteous and good" (Romans 7:12). He judges justly, according to actual desert (Genesis 18:25; Psalms 7:11; 96:13; Acts 17:31). His "wrath," that is, his active judicial hostility to sin, is wholly just in its manifestations (Romans 2:5-16), and his particular "judgments" (retributive punishments) are glorious and praiseworthy (Revelation 16:5, 7; 19:1-4). Whenever God fulfills his covenant commitment by acting to save his people, it is a gesture of "righteousness," that is, justice (Isaiah 51:5-6; 56:1; 63:1; 1 John 1:9). When God justifies sinners through faith in Christ, he does so on the basis of justice done, that is, the punishment of our sins in the person of Christ our substitute; thus the form taken by his justifying mercy shows him to be utterly and totally just (Romans 3:25-26), and our justification itself is shown to be judicially justified.

When John says that God is "light," with no darkness in him at all, the image is affirming God's holy purity, which makes fellowship between him and the willfully unholy impossible and requires the pursuit of holiness and righteousness of life to be a central concern for Christian people (1 John 1:5-2:1; 2 Corinthians 6:14-7:1; Hebrews 12:10-17). The summons to believers, regenerate and forgiven as they are, to practice a holiness that will match God's own, and so please him, is constant in the New Testament, as indeed it was in the Old Testament. Because God is holy, God's people must be holy too.

Concise Theology, pp.43–44

꒰

Holy, holy, holy! Lord God Almighty!
Early in the morning our song shall rise to thee;
Holy, holy, holy! Merciful and mighty!
God in three persons, blessed Trinity!

Holy, holy, holy! All the saints adore thee,
Casting down their golden crowns around the glassy sea;
Cherubim and seraphim falling down before thee,
Which wert, and art, and evermore shalt be.

Holy, holy, holy! Though the darkness hide thee,
Though the eye of sinful man thy glory may not see;
Only thou art holy; there is none beside thee,
Perfect in power, in love, and purity.

Holy, holy, holy, Lord God Almighty!
All thy works shall praise thy name in earth and sky and sea;
Holy, holy, holy, merciful and mighty,
God in three Persons, blessed Trinity!

꒰

REGINALD HEBER

27

Holiness:
How Our Righteous God Behaves

Most of what the Bible says about God's holiness is said in the Old Testament. There, God is often called "the Holy One of Israel," or simply "the Holy One" (e.g., Isaiah 40:25). He swears by his holiness, i.e., by himself and all that he is (Amos 4:2). His "name"—that is, his revealed nature—is regularly spoken of as "holy" (e.g., Isaiah 57:15). The angels worship him by crying "Holy, holy, holy, is the Lord Almighty" (Isaiah 6:3). In the New Testament, references to the divine holiness are less common, but we do on occasion find the word "holy" applied to all three Persons of the Godhead. Christ prays "Holy Father" (John 17:11); the devils identify Christ as "the Holy One of God" (Mark 1:24); and the Comforter's name is the Holy Spirit (the name occurs, in fact, nearly one hundred times).

When God is called "holy," the thought conveyed is that of deity, and more particularly of those qualities of deity which mark out the infinite superiority of the Triune Jehovah over mankind, in respect of both powers and perfections. The word points to God as standing above and apart from men, a different kind of being on a higher plane of existence. It focuses attention on everything in God that makes him a proper object of awe and worship and reverent fear, and that serves to remind his human creatures how ungodlike they really are. Thus it denotes, *first,* God's infinite greatness and power, contrasted with the smallness and weakness of us men and women; *second,* it denotes his perfect purity and uprightness, which stand in glaring contrast with the unrighteousness and uncleanness of sinful humanity, and which call forth from him that inflexible retributive reaction to sin that the Bible calls his "wrath" and "judgment"; *third*, it denotes his determination to maintain his own righteous rule, however much it may be resisted and opposed—a resolve that makes it certain that all sin will eventually receive its due reward. The biblical idea of God's holiness involves all this.

The connection between holiness and judgment on sin is brought out in a verse like Isaiah 5:16, in which Israel is told: "the Lord Almighty will be exalted by his justice, and the holy God will show himself holy by his righteousness." When the holy God asserts himself in righteous judgment against evildoers, then he "is sanctified," i.e., his holiness is revealed and vindicated. The RSV renders, "the Holy God *shows himself holy* in righteousness." Such acts of power and justice declare his greatness and manifest his glory before men: by these means, God makes himself known and gets himself honor. The connection between these things is brought out at the close of another prophecy of judgment (Ezekiel 38:23, RSV): "So I will show my greatness and my holiness and *make myself known* in the eyes of many nations. Then they will know that I am the Lord" [italics mine].

As God sanctifies himself by revealing his holiness in acts of judgment, so in the Old Testament men "sanctify God" when they honor his revelation by reverent observance of his will (see Numbers 20:12; 27:14; Isaiah 8:13). This honoring of God's holiness is the essence of worship. In a parallel sense, Peter exhorts Christians to "in your hearts reverence Christ as Lord" (1 Peter 3:15, RSV). We "sanctify" the Lord Jesus Christ by letting him rule over our lives.

God's holiness, as we have seen, means not only his infinite power, but also what the hymn calls his "awful purity." The holiness to which he calls his people is not an aspiration after the former, but an imitation of the latter. Holiness is the Bible word for man's due response to God as *his* God, within the covenant relationship. God commands those whom he has separated from other peoples to be his people, that they should separate themselves from all that displeases him and is contrary to his will. Holiness of life is what he requires of all those whom he has brought into fellowship with himself.

God's Words, pp.171–72

꒰

In your hearts enthrone him; there let him subdue

All that is not holy, all that is not true;

Crown him as your Captain, in temptation's hour,

Let his will enfold you in its light and power.

꒰

CAROLINE M. NOEL

28

Light and Love:
The Divine Agenda Is Our Sanctification

The triune God is *light*. This means that he is holy—pure and perfect, loving all good and hating all evil. Also, it means that he constantly searches out all that is in us, so that "everything is uncovered and laid bare before the eyes of him to whom we must give account" (Hebrews 4:13). The exposing of what would otherwise lie hidden in darkness is one of the thoughts that the biblical image of *light* regularly conveys, (see John 3:19-21; Ephesians 5:11-14) so no unholiness in us will go unnoticed.

The triune God who is *light* is also *love*—holy love. (See 1 John 1:5; 4:8, 16.) What does this mean? It means that only what is actually holy and worthy can give God actual satisfaction. As the love that binds spouses in a good marriage is an evaluative love that appreciates the excellence of the loved one, so the love that binds Father, Son, and Spirit is an evaluative love whereby each delights in the holiness of the other two, and in the holiness of the holy angels. That love will not have full joy of us who are Christ's until we are holy too. Nor can we fully love God, and fully enjoy him as we love him, while we know ourselves to be still in the grip of moral weaknesses and perversities. To know oneself, here and now, to be, in Luther's phrase, *simul justus et peccator*—a justified sinner, right with God though sinning still—is a wonderful privilege. But the hope set before us is yet more wonderful, namely to be in the presence of God, seeing him and fellowshiping with him, as one who is a sinner no longer. What God plans for us in the present is to lead us toward this goal.

So the divine agenda for the rest of my life on earth is my sanctification. I have been raised from spiritual death and born again in Christ so that I might be changed into his moral likeness. "You were taught," Paul tells me (for I, like all other Bible-readers, stand with the Ephesian Christians at this point), "with regard to your former way of life, to put off your old self ... to be made new ... and to put on the new self, created to be like God in true righteousness and holiness" (Ephesians 4:22-24; see also Colossians 3:9-10). The detailed moral directives in each of Paul's letters show me that he means this in the most literal and down-to-earth sense.

Increasing conformity to the image of Christ—to his righteousness and holiness, his love and humility, his self-denial and single-mindedness, his wisdom and prudence, his boldness and self-control, his faithfulness and strength under pressure—is the sum and substance of the "good works" for which Christians have been created (that is, re-created) in Christ (Ephesians 2:10). It is also the "good" for which in all things God works in the lives of those who love him (Romans 8:28). The God in whose hands I am, willy-nilly, and whom I have in fact gladly and penitently put in charge of my life, is in the holiness business. Part of the answer to the question that life's roller coaster ride repeatedly raises, *why has this happened to me?* is always: it is moral training and discipline, planned by my heavenly Father to help me forward along the path of Christlike virtue.

Rediscovering Holiness, pp.59–61

Eternal light! Eternal light!
How pure the soul must be
When, placed within thy searching sight,
It shrinks not, but with calm delight
Can live and look on thee!

The spirits that surround thy throne
May bear the burning bliss;
But that is surely theirs alone,
Since they have never, never known
A fallen world like this.

O how shall I, whose native sphere
Is dark, whose mind is dim,
Before the ineffable appear,
And on my naked spirit bear
The uncreated beam?

There is a way for man to rise
To that sublime abode—
An offering and a sacrifice,
The Holy Spirit's energies,
An advocate with God.

These, these prepare us for the sight
Of holiness above;
The sons of ignorance and night
May dwell in the eternal light
Through the eternal love.

THOMAS BINNEY

29

Wrath and Mercy:
God Makes Peace with His Enemies

God is at enmity with sinners. This has been often denied, but the Bible is in no doubt about it. We were reconciled to God through the death of Christ "while we were *enemies*," says Paul in Romans 5:10, and commentators of all schools agree that this term here signifies as part, if not all, of its meaning "objects of divine hostility," which the context certainly seems to demand. "The word *enemies* is applied to men not only as descriptive of their moral character, but also of the relation in which they stand to God as the objects of his displeasure. There is not only a wicked opposition of the sinner to God, but a holy opposition of God to the sinner" (C. Hodge, *Romans*, p. 136). Again, says Paul, we were all "by nature *objects of wrath*" (Ephesians 2:3), heirs of the vengeance that God has proclaimed against those who transgress his laws.

The biblical idea of the wrath of God is well defined by James Orr: it is "an energy of the divine nature called forth by the presence of daring or presumptuous transgression, and expressing the reaction of the divine holiness against it in the punishment or destruction of the transgressor. It is the 'zeal' of God for the maintenance of His holiness and honour, and of the ends of His righteousness and love, when these are threatened by the ingratitude, rebellion and willful disobedience or temerity of the creature" (Hastings' *Dictionary of the Bible*, I, pp. 77ff.). God's wrath against sin is not a fitful flicker, but a steady blaze; not a mark of uncertain temper, but an aspect of the consistent righteousness of the just Judge of all the earth. To this hostile reaction of God, Paul tells us, all sinners, as such, are exposed. The first truth expounded in Romans is that "the wrath of God is being revealed from heaven against all the godlessness and wickedness of men" (Romans 1:18). The background of the good news of grace is the bad news of judgment; the context within which the New Testament announces God's reconciling mercy is the declaration of his active wrath. Humans are opposed to God in their sin, and God is opposed to humans in his holiness. Those who are under the rule of sin are also under the wrath of God. It is against the dark backcloth of this view of the natural relations of man and his Maker that the gospel of reconciliation is expounded.

Reconciliation means peacemaking: and Christ made peace, we are told, "through his blood shed on the cross" (Colossians 1:20). "We were reconciled to him through the death of his Son" (Romans 5:10). How are we to understand this? We cannot here go fully into Paul's view of the atonement, but we may make three points that spring directly from the texts that we are studying.

1. Reconciliation was made, we are told, through the *blood* of Christ (Colossians 1:20). This points to the thought of *sacrifice*, according to the Old Testament pattern that required the shedding of blood for the remission of guilt.

2. Paul's analysis of the meaning of reconciliation is that through the blood-shedding of Christ, peace was made between God and humans (Colossians 1:20), the enmity between them was destroyed (Romans 5:10; Ephesians 2:16), and the divine wrath was turned away from them forever (Romans 5:9-10). This points to the thought of *propitiation;* indeed, "propitiation" is defined as the turning away of God's wrath, and is no more than a technical name for the reconciling, pacificatory effects of the cross as described above.

3. God reconciled the world to himself, says Paul, by means of a judicial exchange: "For our sake he made him to be sin who knew no sin, so that in him we might become the righteousness of God" (2 Corinthians 5:21, RSV). Paul has just affirmed that reconciliation means the non-imputation of their trespasses to the trespassers; here he shows that the ground of this non-imputation is the imputing of their trespasses to Christ, and his bearing God's holy reaction to them. As Paul says in Galatians 3:13, "Christ redeemed us from the curse of the law by becoming a curse for us." The reason why we do not have to bear our own sins is that Christ bore them in our place. This points to the thought of *substitution*.

It was, then, by a substitutionary, propitiatory sacrifice on the part of the sinless Son of God that our reconciliation was achieved. So much did salvation cost; and it was for God's enemies that this price was paid. "Christ died for the ungodly ... God demonstrates his own love for us in this: While we were still sinners, Christ died for us" (Romans 5:6, 8). God quenched and put away his own just wrath against us by sending his own Son to atone for our sins in the darkness of Calvary. It is this that teaches us the measure of the mercy of God; this that shows us the meaning of "God is love."

God's Words, pp.123–25

꒰

My song is love unknown, my Savior's love to me,

love to the loveless shown that they might lovely be.

O who am I that for my sake

my Lord should take frail flesh, and die?

He came from his blest throne salvation to bestow,

but men made strange, and none the longed-for Christ

would know.

But O my friend, my friend indeed,

who at my need his life did spend.

꒰

SAMUEL CROSSMAN

30

Forgiveness:
God Pardons Us So We Can Pardon Others

The Christian lives through forgiveness. This is what justification by faith is all about. We could have no life or hope with God at all, had God's Son not borne the penalty for our sins so that we might go free. But Christians fall short still, and forgiveness is needed each day; so Jesus in part two of his model prayer included a request for it between the pleas for material provision and spiritual protection. This reflects nothing in his own praying, for he knew he was sinless; it is here for us.

How should Christians see their sins? Scripture presents sins as lawbreaking, deviation, shortcoming, rebellion, pollution (dirt), and missing one's target, and it is always all these things in relation to God; but the special angle from which the Lord's Prayer views it is that of unpaid debts. "Forgive us our debts, as we also have forgiven our debtors" is the RSV rendering of Matthew 6:12. Those denominations that say "trespasses" instead of "debts," echoing Luke 11:4, unfortunately miss this point. Jesus' thought is that we owe God total tireless loyalty—zealous love for God and men, all day and every day, on the pattern of Jesus' own—and our sin is basically failure to pay. The Anglican Prayer Book rightly confesses sins of omission ("we have left undone those things which we ought to have done") before sins of commission: the omission perspective is basic. When Christians examine themselves, it is for omissions that they should first look, and they will always find that their saddest sins take the form of good left undone. When the dying Archbishop Usher prayed, "Lord, forgive most of all my sins of omission," he showed a true sense of spiritual reality.

A problem arises here. If Christ's death atoned for all sins, past, present, and future (as it did), and if God's verdict justifying the believer ("I accept you as righteous for Jesus' sake") is eternally valid (as it is), why need the Christian mention his daily sins to God at all? The answer lies in distinguishing between God as Judge and as Father, and between being a justified sinner and an adopted son. The Lord's Prayer is the family prayer, in which God's adopted children address their Father, and though their daily failures do not overthrow their justification, things will not be right between them and their Father till they have said "sorry" and asked him to overlook the ways they have let him down. Unless Christians come to God each time as returning prodigals, their prayer will be as unreal as was that of the Pharisee in Jesus' parable.

Here emerges a lesson: Christians must be willing to examine themselves and let others examine them for the detecting of day-to-day shortcomings. The Puritans valued preachers who would "rip up" the conscience; more such preaching is needed today. The discipline of self-examination, though distasteful to our pride, is necessary because our holy Father in heaven will not turn a blind eye to his children's failings, as human parents so often (and so unwisely) do. So what he knows about our sins we need to know too, so that we may repent and ask pardon for whatever has given offense.

From one standpoint, Christians' shortcomings offend most of all, just because they have most reason (the love of God in Christ) and most resources (the indwelling Holy Spirit) for avoiding sinful ways. Those who think that because in Christ their sins are covered they need not bother to keep God's law are desperately confused (see Romans 6). As it upsets a man more to learn that his wife is sleeping around than that the girl next door is doing it, so God is most deeply outraged when his own people are unfaithful (see Hosea's prophecy, especially chapters 1–3). "This is the will of God, your sanctification" (1 Thessalonians 4:3, RSV)—and nothing less will do.

The Communion Service in the 1662 Prayer Book teaches Christians to call the "burden" (guilt) of their sins "intolerable." The justification for this strong language is knowledge of the intolerable grief brought to God by the sins of his own family. How sensitive are we to this? And how concerned that, as sons of God, our lives should be so far as possible sin-free? The true Christian will not only seek to find and face his sins through self-examination, but he will labor "by the Spirit" to "put to death the misdeeds of the body" (i.e., the habits of the old sinful self) all his days (Romans 8:13).

Those who hope for God's forgiveness, said Jesus, must be able to tell him that they too have forgiven their debtors. This is not a matter of earning forgiveness by works but of qualifying for it by repentance. Repentance—change of mind—makes mercy and forbearance central to one's life-style. Those who live by God's forgiveness must imitate it; one whose only hope is that God will not hold his faults against him forfeits his right to hold others' faults against them. Do as you would be done by is the rule here, and the unforgiving Christian brands himself a hypocrite. It is true that forgiveness is by faith in Christ alone, apart from works, but repentance is faith's fruit, and there is no more reality in a profession of faith than there is reality of repentance accompanying it. Jesus himself stresses that only those who grant forgiveness will receive it in Matthew 6:14ff.; 18:35.

So again the question is: can I say the Lord's Prayer? Can you? We shall all do well to make the following lines a plea of our own.

Growing in Christ, pp.191–94

∽

"Forgive our sins as we forgive,"
—you taught us, Lord, to pray;
but you alone can grant us grace
to live the words we say.

How can your pardon reach and bless
the unforgiving heart
that broods on wrongs, and will not let
old bitterness depart?

In blazing light your Cross reveals
the truth we dimly knew,
how small the debts men owe to us,
how great our debt to you.

Lord, cleanse the depths within our souls,
and bid resentment cease;
then, reconciled to God and man,
our lives will spread your peace.

∽

ROSAMOND E. HERKLOTS

31

Fatherhood:
God Loves His Adopted Children

The Lord's Prayer is in family terms: Jesus teaches us to invoke God as our Father, just as he himself did—witness his Gethsemane prayer, for instance, or his High Priestly prayer in John 17, where the word "Father" appears six times. A question, however, arises. Jesus was God's Son by nature, the second person of the eternal Godhead. We, by contrast, are God's creatures. By what right, then, may we call God *Father?* When Jesus taught this manner of address, was he implying that creaturehood, as such, involves sonship—or what?

Clarity here is vital. Jesus' point, as we saw in an earlier study, is not that all people are God's children by nature, but that his committed disciples have been adopted into God's family by grace. "To all who received him, who believed in his name, he gave power to become children of God" (John 1:12, RSV). Paul states this as the purpose of the incarnation: "God sent forth his Son ... so that we might receive adoption as sons" (Galatians 4:4, 5, RSV). Prayer to God as Father is for Christians only.

This resolves a puzzle. Elsewhere, Jesus stressed that his disciples should pray in his name and through him; that is, looking to him as our way of access to the Father. (See John 14:6, 13; 15:16; 16:23-26.) Why is there none of this in the model prayer? In fact, the point is present here; it is implicit in "Father." Only those who look to Jesus as Mediator and sin-bearer, and go to God through him, have any right to call on God as his sons.

If we are to pray and live as we should, we must grasp the implications of God's gracious fatherhood.

First, as God's adopted children we are *loved* no less than is the one whom God called his "beloved Son" (Matthew 3:17; 17:5, RSV). In some families containing biological and adopted children, the former are favored above the latter, but no such defect mars the fatherhood of God.

This is the best news anyone has ever heard. It means that, as Paul triumphantly declares, nothing "... in all creation, will be able to separate us from the love of God that is in Christ Jesus our Lord" (Romans 8:39). It means that God will never forget us, or cease to care for us, and that he remains our forbearing Father even when we act the prodigal (as, alas, we all sometimes do).

It means, too, that, as the Prayer Books say, he is "always more ready to hear than we to pray," and is "wont to give more than either we desire or deserve." "If you, then, though you are evil," said our Lord, "know how to give good gifts to your children, how much more will your Father in heaven give good gifts to those who ask him!" (Matthew 7:11; the parallel saying in Luke 11:13 has "Holy Spirit" for "good things," and the sustained ministry of the Holy Spirit was surely one of the good things Jesus had in mind). To know this truth of God's fatherly love to us gives boundless confidence not merely for praying, but for all our living.

Second, we are God's *heirs*. Adoption in the ancient world was for securing an heir, and Christians are joint heirs with Christ of God's glory (Romans 8:17). "We are God's children now ... when he appears we shall be like him" (1 John 3:2, RSV). Already "all things are yours" in the sense that they further your good here and your glory hereafter, for "you are Christ's" (1 Corinthians 3:21-23, RSV). To grasp this is to know oneself rich and privileged beyond any monarch or millionaire.

Third, we have *God's Spirit* in us. With our changed relationship to God (adoption) goes a change of direction and desire, of outlook and attitude, that Scripture calls regeneration or new birth. Those who "believed in" Jesus' "name" were "born ... of God" (John 1:12ff.), or more precisely, "born of the Spirit" (3:6; see verses 3-8). "Because you are sons," says Paul, "God has sent the Spirit of his Son into our hearts, crying [that is, prompting us to cry, spontaneously, as the expression of a new spiritual instinct], 'Abba! Father!'" (Galatians 4:6, RSV). And when, to our distress (and this comes to us all), we find ourselves so muddle-headed, dead-hearted, and tongue-tied in prayer that "we do not know how to pray as we ought," then our very desire to pray as we should and our grief that we are not doing so shows that the Spirit is himself making effective intercession for us in our hearts (Romans 8:26ff., RSV); which is as reassuring as it is mysterious, and as thrilling as it is amazing.

Fourth, we must *honor* our Father by serving his interests. The center of our concern must be "thy name ... kingdom ... will," and we must be like good children in human families, ready to obey instructions.

Fifth, we must love our *brothers,* by constant care and prayer for them. The Lord's Prayer schools us in intercession for the family's needs: "Our Father ... give us ... forgive us ... lead us ... deliver us...." "Us" means more than just me! For God's child, prayer is no "flight of the alone to the Alone," but concern for the family is built into it.

So we should be expressing faith in Christ, confidence in God, joy in the Holy Spirit, a purpose of obedience, and concern for our fellow Christians when we go to God and call him "Father." Only so shall we answer Jesus' intention in teaching us this form of address.

As invocation of God as Father opens this pattern prayer, so renewed realization of the family relationship—his parenthood, and our sonship by grace—should always come first in our practice of prayer. All right-minded praying starts with a long look Godward and a deliberate lifting up of one's heart to give thanks and adore, and it is just this that "Father" calls us to. Thanks for grace, and praise for God's paternity, and joy in our sonship and heirship should bulk large in Christian prayer, and if we never got beyond it we should still be praying to good purpose. First things first!

So I ask: Do we always pray to God as Father? And do we always praise when we pray?

Growing in Christ, pp.163–66

ॐ

Children of the heavenly Father
Safely in his bosom gather;
Nestling bird nor star in heaven
Such a refuge e'er was given.

Neither life nor death shall ever
From the Lord his children sever;
Unto them his grace he showeth,
And their sorrows all he knoweth.

Though he giveth or he taketh,
God his children ne'er forsaketh;
His the loving purpose solely
To preserve them pure and holy.

ॐ

LINA SANDELL

Bibliography

Concise Theology. Wheaton, Ill.: Tyndale, 1993.

God Has Spoken. Grand Rapids, Mich.: Baker, 1979, 1993.

God's Words. Grand Rapids, Mich.: Baker, 1988.

Growing in Christ. Wheaton, Ill.: Crossway, 1994.

Knowing Christianity. Wheaton, Ill.: Harold Shaw, 1995.

Knowing God. Downers Grove, Ill.: InterVarsity, 1973.

Rediscovering Holiness. Ann Arbor, Mich.: Servant, 1992.

"The Trinity and the Gospel," *Good News for All Seasons*, Richard Allen Bodey, ed., Grand Rapids, Mich.: Baker, 1987.